Practising Public

Antipode Book Series

General Editor: Noel Castree, Professor of Geography, University of Manchester, UK

Like its parent journal, the Antipode Book Series reflects distinctive new developments in radical geography. It publishes books in a variety of formats – from reference books to works of broad explication to titles that develop and extend the scholarly research base – but the commitment is always the same: to contribute to the praxis of a new and more just society.

Published

Practising Public Scholarship: Experiences and Possibilities Beyond the Academy
Edited by Katharyne Mitchell

Grounding Globalization: Labour in the Age of Insecurity
Edward Webster, Rob Lambert and Andries Bezuidenhout

Privatization: Property and the Remaking of Nature-Society Relations
Edited by Becky Mansfield

Decolonizing Development: Colonial Power and the Maya
Joel Wainwright

Cities of Whiteness
Wendy S. Shaw

Neoliberalization: States, Networks, Peoples
Edited by Kim England and Kevin Ward

The Dirty Work of Neoliberalism: Cleaners in the Global Economy
Edited by Luis L. M. Aguiar and Andrew Herod

David Harvey: A Critical Reader
Edited by Noel Castree and Derek Gregory

Working the Spaces of Neoliberalism: Activism, Professionalisation and Incorporation
Edited by Nina Laurie and Liz Bondi

Threads of Labour: Garment Industry Supply Chains from the Workers' Perspective
Edited by Angela Hale and Jane Wills

Life's Work: Geographies of Social Reproduction
Edited by Katharyne Mitchell, Sallie A. Marston and Cindi Katz

Redundant Masculinities? Employment Change and White Working Class Youth
Linda McDowell

Spaces of Neoliberalism
Edited by Neil Brenner and Nik Theodore

Space, Place and the New Labour Internationalism
Edited by Peter Waterman and Jane Wills

Forthcoming

Working Places: Property, Nature and the Political Possibilities of Community Land Ownership
Fiona D. Mackenzie

Practising Public Scholarship

Experiences and Possibilities Beyond the Academy

Edited by

Katharyne Mitchell

⊗WILEY-BLACKWELL

A John Wiley & Sons, Ltd., Publication

This edition first published 2008
Chapters © 2008 the Authors
Book Compilation © 2008 Editorial Board of Antipode and Blackwell Publishing Ltd
First published as volume 40, issue 3 of *Antipode*

Blackwell Publishing was acquired by John Wiley & Sons in February 2007. Blackwell's publishing program has been merged with Wiley's global Scientific, Technical, and Medical business to form Wiley-Blackwell.

Registered Office

John Wiley & Sons Ltd, The Atrium, Southern Gate, Chichester, West Sussex, PO19 8SQ, United Kingdom

Editorial Offices

350 Main Street, Malden, MA 02148-5020, USA
9600 Garsington Road, Oxford, OX4 2DQ, UK
The Atrium, Southern Gate, Chichester, West Sussex, PO19 8SQ, UK

For details of our global editorial offices, for customer services, and for information about how to apply for permission to reuse the copyright material in this book please see our website at www.wiley.com/wiley-blackwell.

Library of Congress Cataloging-in-Publication Data

Practising public scholarship : experiences and possibilities beyond the academy / edited by Katharyne Mitchell.
p. cm. – (Antipode book series)
Includes bibliographical references and index.
ISBN 978-1-4051-8912-5 (pbk. : alk. paper)
1. Community and college.
2. Universities and colleges–Public services. 3. Learning and scholarship. I. Mitchell, Katharyne.
LC237.P73 2008
378.1'03–dc22

2008027428

A catalogue record for this book is available from the British Library.

Set in 10.5pt Times
by Aptara, New Delhi, India
Printed in Singapore
by Fabulous Printers Pte Ltd

01 2008

In memory of Allan Pred

Contents

Introduction: Becoming Political

Katharyne Mitchell

Soon after finishing graduate school I told an eminent person in our field that I would like our incipient scholarly collaboration to have some political relevance. He responded with a raised eyebrow, "I don't know what you mean by 'political'". It was a crafty response and I recall being paralyzed by it. What does it mean to be political in academic life? Why was I so sure that I already knew? Did that assurance cast doubt on my potential as an intellectual? By desiring a project with political relevance was I showing myself to be both close-minded and theoretically naïve, the equivalent of a somewhat dense academic bigot?

I have subsequently spent a fair number of hours pondering the meaning of "political" and in some ways I feel that I have returned to my starting point. Yet the journey itself has been instructive, and even if it began with a sly postmodern push in the small of the back, I'm glad I made it. For many people working in the academy, the last couple of decades have brought an intoxicating brew of fresh ideas across the social sciences and humanities, a brew that has—and I'm speaking very generally here—caused a widespread rethinking of the nature of knowledge and the representation of reality. The idea that certain claims and judgments accurately reflect a pre-given reality (existing prior to the researcher/interpreter's arrival) was persuasively critiqued by those arguing for the contingency and social construction of all knowledge. Foundationalist thought of all stripes and hues was soon placed on the chopping block, leading to a veritable orgy of destruction and dismemberment. It was extremely satisfying at first, all of those functionalist limbs and structuralist torsos lying about, fragmented and nonlinear. But while liberating in many ways, this initial heady period led to a dispiriting state of paralysis for quite a few good souls, and I remember more than one graduate seminar in which I felt that the language of "transient articulations" and "emergent multiplicities" was going to drive me mad.

The problem was further entrenched by the perceived loss of the moral language of "rights". As Cary Wolf has noted, "almost all progressive movements (and some not so progressive ones) find it effective to trade upon the rhetoric of 'rights'".[1] What is a politically minded person to do, when it becomes clear that the idea of human rights carries unacceptable historical baggage, connected as it is with a violent and exclusionary liberal lineage, one with a cheery but ultimately false notion of equal rights under the law? This is not even to mention the hideous possibility of retaining a concept of "the human".

Many students dropped the language of human rights as if it had turned around and bitten them on the hand. But they neglected to pick up anything else, and it often seemed to me that the more people read and understood, the less claims they felt able to make; the sharper and stronger their tools of analysis, the less there was to defend or construct. For those working in the sciences, critiques of claims to truth often seemed to encompass the entire scientific project, leaving scant room to negotiate a middle ground, and ultimately repelling many critical and sympathetic allies. In the rush to attack anything smacking of a pre-given structure or even worse "metanarrative", what often got lost was a broad and inclusive notion of the political, and with it a sense of voice and purpose.

What does it mean to be political? And why does this feel like an intuitive rather than an intellectual question? My sense is that what creates a public scholar is related to a profound urge to participate and intervene in the political practices of the world—to fight injustice or correct misinformation or provide a needed service—in short, to try to make the world a better place, corny as that sounds. But is this desire compatible with an academic project? Does it necessarily involve selling out, either intellectually, personally or politically?

Like many public scholars I have both spoken and written for audiences outside of a university setting. In just about every situation that I can recall, I have radically changed my language, including the vocabulary and even grammatical structure of my sentences. But I have retained most, if not all, of the content, and in a number of cases, I have felt that editorial suggestions made my writing crisper and stronger than the original draft. I've found it surprisingly easy to jettison words like neoliberalism without losing the thread of my argument, and I've also found audiences generally receptive to critiques of free-market capitalism, even though I rarely use words like capitalism, which has a different resonance inside and outside of the university.

But even so there are some boundaries I don't cross and some self-censorship that I perform, partly out of the desire to hold onto my audience and partly from naked fear. It's different speaking or writing to people who don't necessarily share your intellectual or political positions or even ascribe much to your right to espouse them. And knowing that you will need to defend everything you claim clearly and forcefully is a lot scarier than resting secure in your knowledge that everything is "complicated" (all of those emergent multiplicities), and surely the questioner must understand that too? Is it selling out to perform these small censoring moves?

I find these compromises relatively minor in the larger scheme of things, and I do not agree with Wolf's characterization of the public intellectual's internal psyche as one of profound schizophrenia. (The result of a supposed discrepancy between theoretical belief, eg in opposition to foundationalist concepts, and the necessity to invoke those same concepts in order to be politically efficacious in the public arena.) The only time that I have felt somewhat queasy in this regard is when I have advocated for the "rights" of middle-class children to be spared the bruising and competitive scramble for that elusive place at Harvard or Yale and taught instead to be those gentle and cooperative citizens we'd much rather have in our classrooms and our world. But really my trepidation here is not so much related to an intellectual sell-out, ie my invocation of rights, or the idea that there is such a thing as a child, or even the liberal panacea to what is obviously a systemic problem. Rather, my sell-out here is profoundly political: why am I talking about middle-class American children's problems to begin with, when their problems are relatively minor compared with those of most of the rest of the world?

I don't suffer from intellectual schizophrenia, possibly because I hold some semi-foundational (if there is such a thing) beliefs about the contemporary workings of the world: for example, that there's a widely entrenched and increasingly hegemonic socio-economic system that is making a few people exceedingly rich and a lot of people extremely poor; and that most societies are dominated by men and this has negative repercussions for both men and women. I don't think these processes are natural or inevitable or irretrievable, and, *pace* Wolf, the main "rights" I need to invoke to counteract them long predate liberalism. So this gives me hope and intellectual cover. But if I'm truly honest, it also gives me a deep sense of personal inadequacy. Rome is burning, and I'm organizing workshops and writing about American children? Unequal education systems? Gentrification? The spatial banishment of prostitutes? What I do as an academic never seems important enough, or just *enough*. But I suppose, as David Domke says in this book, it's the something I can do, at least for now.

Most of the authors in this book were pulled into public scholarship rather than seeking it out. But in all of the essays you sense a profound pleasure in what has come to pass, one that outweighs any initial feelings of trepidation. Each person has found his or her own way of waging scholarship in difficult times. Scholar-activists retain a passion for the political grassroots campaigns they joined in their youth; scholarly producers organize collaborative ventures, make plans, find money, start institutions, and generally just get things up and running; public intellectuals make their research and ideas accessible through media contacts, public outreach, writing for the newspapers, making videos, and endlessly soliciting all possible outlets for informing the wider community about their political and intellectual passions; critical scholar-pedagogues take their classrooms out of the university and bring the outer world in, make connections with K-12 schools, rewrite curricula, and conduct their research and their lives with the same democratic spirit in which they run their classes; scholar-politicos enter the political arena itself, running their campaigns with ideas and ideals rather than via sound bites.

These projects have not come without personal cost. The personal implications vary, but each contributor has experienced some negative moments along with the highlights. These include those whose work has been impugned as "non-objective", whose careers have been threatened or derailed, whose academic papers have been withdrawn, and/or whose colleagues have scorned or demoted them.

Many important public voices in the world are not evident in this volume precisely because of these kinds of personal and political difficulties. The costs of remaining affiliated with university systems are often too great for many public intellectuals, who have chosen, or been forced, to opt out of academia altogether. There are many reasons for these types of difficulties, which vary greatly both within countries and regions, as well as more broadly between western and non-western settings. Faculty in university systems in the US, Canada, and the UK, for example, are under increasing pressure to produce more books and articles in shorter periods of time, thus decreasing the opportunities to engage in activities outside of the standardized, narrowly circumscribed ideals of their disciplines and departments. These pressures are part of the broad shift to an increasingly market-based logic that has infiltrated and affected most university systems over the past few decades.[2] This logic makes university life increasingly incompatible with the social and political projects of many potential scholars, and has reduced the number of public intellectuals operating within academic settings. For many other public intellectuals, especially those working in politically unstable venues, political considerations are primary in their decisions to leave the university. Academic affiliations end up either impeding their work or becoming impossible to maintain in the face of political opposition both within and outside the university.

This book is not a general collection of works by prominent public intellectuals such as these. Neither is it an exegesis on the meaning of public scholarship, although there are a good number of insights that can be gleaned throughout the texts.[3] Rather, the essays here are deeply personal accounts about the journey to becoming a public scholar and to intervening politically in the world, *while remaining within a university system*. All of the essayists consider themselves academics but also something more. That little bit more is integral to the person's identity and core; it influences—whether consciously or not—the types of research questions asked, experiments or fieldwork pursued, clinics or centers established, and contacts made and maintained. It also gives these writers a sense of personal power, and a belief that their actions can and do make a difference.

When I invited contributions to this book I was delighted by the positive response. Although busy, tired, overworked, overcommitted, and then some, each of these essayists wanted to reach out and provide a manifesto and a road map so that others could follow in their footsteps. Within these pages are intellectual biographies and also calls to action from academics across the disciplinary spectrum. They are unique but also share any number of meditative thoughts among them. One recurring emotion that pervades the essays is a general sense of shock and dismay that so few people in academia use their professional authority to make their voices count. Hence as these authors narrate their lives and ideas, you might detect a seductive invitation that runs through every essay: *join us*.

Endnotes

[1] Cary Wolf, "Getting the dirt on the public intellectual: a response to Michael Bérubé", *ebr2*. See http://www.altx.com/ebr/ebr2/2wolfe.htm
[2] On the theme of the increasing corporatization of the university, see Readings (1997).
[3] For a more "intellectual" discussion of the meaning of the public intellectual, see Small (2002).

References

Readings B (1997) *The University in Ruins*. Cambridge, MA: Harvard University Press.
Small H (2002) *The Public Intellectual*. Oxford: Wiley-Blackwell.

Chapter 1
Comrades and Colons

Terry Eagleton

Perhaps my finest contribution to the general welfare of humanity as a public intellectual involved the correct handling of the colon. I was a member at the time of a far-left political group in Oxford—a fact which seemed to occasion a number of rather strange clickings and whirrings whenever I picked up the phone, and involved an extraordinary number of visits to my local telegraph pole by workmen apparently repairing the line. One of the senior members of the group was a shop steward at what was then the largest automobile plant in the south of England, and had a long career of industrial militancy. The company would have dearly loved to dismiss him, and finally seized the chance to do so when he parked his car illegally for 30 seconds or so outside their gates. For some years he had been writing a history of the workers' fight for better conditions at the plant, a piece of work which constituted a precious addition to the annals of the English labour and socialist movements. But he was handier with a megaphone than he was with the intricacies of English grammar, and finally handed the manuscript over to me to knock into syntactical shape. I spent a number of lonely evenings embroiled in the revolutionary struggle to turn commas into colons, introduce some elementary paragraphing into a seamless text, and find synonyms for "bosses" and "shameful betrayal". We had to fight hard to find the book a publisher, but were finally successful.

While engaged on this world-historical literary task in the evenings, I was teaching Oxford English undergraduates during the day about the heroic couplet in Alexander Pope and the influence of Schopenhauer on Conrad. I was doing this partly because I had earlier passed up the opportunity to become what I suppose one might call a full-time public intellectual. Just as I was finishing an entirely useless piece of doctoral research at Cambridge in the mid-1960s, the then Labour government in Britain set up what was known at the time as the University of the Air, and which was soon to alter this rather ethereal title to the more sober "Open University". The university offers degrees to so-called "mature" students who for one reason or another have missed out on a college education, and teaches them partly through radio and television. I was unofficially offered a job there, but I was offered an Oxford Fellowship at the same time; and though I already felt at the tender age of 23 that I had had enough of the ivory tower to last me a lifetime, the more politically attractive alternative of the Open University was also much more precarious. It was a fiercely contentious project at the time, closely identified with the left, and there was a general feeling that the Conservatives would wind it up when they returned to office. Since Oxford colleges are about as unlikely to pack up as the sun, I ignominiously opted for the safer bet over the more exciting one. The Open University did not in the event pack up, and I went on to do a good deal of work for it when I wasn't talking about Schopenhauer.

What is the difference between an academic and an intellectual? In one sense, the two terms are almost antithetical. Academics, for example, tend to restrict their labours to surreally narrow fields. I once came across a doctoral thesis in Cambridge entitled "Some aspects of the vaginal system of the flea". ("Some aspects" is appealingly English in its modest self-effacement: nothing too brash, ambitious or distastefully transatlantic.) Intellectuals, on the other hand, tend to shift promiscuously from one subject area to another. Quite how would one label Jürgen Habermas, Julia Kristeva or the late Edward Said? But the versatility of the intellectual, which may involve a certain generic and stylistic versatility as well, doesn't exist for its own sake. Intellectuals need to be fluent in more than one academic discourse if they are to be *public* intellectuals—which is to say, if they want to bring ideas to bear on the political culture as a whole. The intellectual range, in other words, is determined by the social function—for the word "intellectual" denotes a social function rather than a personal characteristic. It doesn't mean "very clever". There are dim intellectuals just as there are bright shop stewards.

So there are three distinct categories at stake here: academics, intellectuals, and public intellectuals. One might claim that Walter Pater was an intellectual, but not exactly a public intellectual in the manner of John Ruskin, John Stuart Mill, Bertrand Russell, Susan Sontag or Umberto Eco. Not all intellectuals appear on television, and the fact that it had not yet been invented is not the only reason why we would not associate the name of Walter Pater with it. The three categories aren't always mutually exclusive. Medics who specialise in the effects of radiation may be academics, but when they campaign against nuclear power plants they are behaving as public intellectuals. Moral philosophers who are drafted in by governments to advise on social ethics are academics-turned-public intellectuals.

Public intellectuals are at their most useful when they find some way of bringing their particular academic expertise to bear on a matter of public importance. Some would claim that they are least useful when they exploit the fact that they have published on Verlaine or flea's vaginas to pontificate about ethnic difference or global warming. Why exactly should we regard Jean-Paul Sartre's comments on Stalinism as necessarily more attention worthy than anyone else's? Because he was an intellectual, and therefore exceptionally intelligent? But I have just suggested that exceptional intelligence is not a *sine qua non* of being an intellectual, as it most definitely is not of being an academic. Why should what poets and novelists have to say about free speech be more worth listening to than what hairdressers have to say about it? I think that there is, in fact, a point in paying special heed to such literary voices on such questions, even though what some of them say may well prove less persuasive than the opinions of hairdressers. For writers are compelled by their trade to have a particular concern with such issues, and are understandably more likely to be scandalised and impassioned when such civil liberties are brutally denied. They also tend to have well-recognised names and are handy with a pen, which is perhaps another reason why they should lend their support to public campaigns.

What is less obviously true, I think, is the proposition that artists, critics and humanities types in general speak from a certain privileged position when it comes to, say, torture and genocide, and have a particular responsibility to intervene in such affairs. One can, to be sure, see the logic of such a case, since it might be thought that a lifetime brooding upon questions of human value equips one to be a more relevant political commentator in such circumstances than a lifetime spent brooding upon algebraic topology or the mating habits of the mongoose. Even so, it carries the rather offensive implication that algebraic topologists are less sensitive and rousable to moral outrage than people who pass their time reading Goethe; and we happen to know from experience that plenty of people who pass their time reading Goethe have about as much moral sensitivity as a drainpipe.

So the question of whether there is a direct link of *this* kind between the humanities and politics—one which might then enable the literary academic to make an "organic" transition to public intellectual—is, I think, still an open one. What is surely not in doubt, however, is that such a connection is not essential for that transition to be successful. It is not essential because in addition to the three categories I have listed there is a fourth one as well, which is that of the citizen. To draw on one's political expertise to speak to a mass rally against the Iraq war is to act as a public intellectual; simply to march in the demonstration is to behave as a citizen. (I myself occupy yet a third category, having more than once spoken in public against the Iraq war without any political expertise on the subject; but then ignorance has never deterred me from anything.)

Even intellectuals, in short, are people as well, hard though it occasionally is to credit. To find a way of placing one's specific talents at the service of a social or political cause is no doubt the ideal or prototypical way for academics to turn themselves into actors in the public arena, even if it involves nothing more grandiose than correcting a working-class militant's spelling. But you can also simply be an academic *and* an actor in the public arena, since it is not likely that more internal relations between politics and what you do in the classroom will crop up all that often. Most of my own activity in political groups has been donkeywork, just like any other members. (It is, however, notable that all members of the political groups I myself have been associated with have been regarded as intellectuals, whatever their background and education. All comrades are expected to attain a certain level of theoretical proficiency. The distinction between worker and intellectual in society at large is overcome within such organisations.) It does not happen all that often, however, that the struggle to keep open a playgroup that the local council is trying to close down urgently needs to sort out the precise relation between Lukács's aesthetics and his epistemology. There is little enough organic relationship between Sartre's notion of the *etre-pour-soi* and his views on Algeria, just as there is no very obvious oblique relation between Habermas's opinion of Nietzsche and his current war-mongering championship of NATO.

One should not, in other words, expect theory and practice to dance a harmonious minuet hand-in-hand throughout history. The relations between them, rather, alter along with that history. There are times (one thinks of the early, enthralling years of the Soviet republic) when theory has to hobble very hard indeed to catch up with a political practice which appears to be shifting from day to day. There are other times, as I was once advised on coming to teach at a US university in the southern states, when if you speak about communism on the campus the students will flock to your classes, whereas if you mention it downtown they will shoot you through the head. What has changed in this respect since the 1960s and 1970s is not that in those halcyon days they were all Althusserians downtown as well. It is rather that, in Europe at least, there existed a political culture beyond the campus with which radical ideas seemed in a general way to resonate, which is not to say that they were necessarily embraced with open arms. This naturally makes it harder for politically conscious academics and graduate students *as such* to find today some public correlative of their theoretical interests; but it does not make it harder to engage with politics simply as citizens, other than in the sense that such forms of engagement have become in general less easy to discover.

One of my own such occasional outlets has been working in the theatre. If literary academics seek to turn their hand to so-called creative writing, they should always choose theatre rather than poetry or the novel because it gets them out of the house. It is a different mode of cultural production altogether, one which in its practical, collective, revisionary, experimental character resembles the scientific laboratory rather more than it does the scholar's study. It is also a suitably chastening experience for intellectuals, since actors have far more respect for the director or lighting designer or even the costume designer than they do for the playwright. One's role for the most part is to sit meekly at the back of the theatre or rehearsal room and watch one's precious creation being estranged before one's eyes. It is also a matter of chasing around the country on the heels of the tour, trying to smuggle in bits of the script which have unaccountably dropped off, or rewriting on the hoof a handful of lines which didn't go down too well in Galway the evening before. If I myself have been able to break out of the cloisters in this way, however, it is largely because I live in Ireland, a country which can boast almost more theatre groups than statues of the Sacred Heart, and in which there is a longstanding liaison between theatre and politics. The theatre groups for which I have worked have been mostly based in the north of the island, and thus with a close relation to political issues.

I mention this not simply as a matter of autobiography, however, but to make a more general point, one which is at once simple-minded and materialist. How far one can be active as a public intellectual depends on one's time and place. It is not something which, in some access of epistemological idealism, we can legislate into existence for ourselves. It is not simply a question of trying harder. In the end, political intellectuals are bred by political movements. It was the fact that Weimar Germany had a flourishing working-class movement, furnished with its own theatres, newspapers and cultural activities, which helped to make possible writers like Bertolt Brecht and Walter Benjamin, just as it was Bolshevism which threw up the Futurists, Formalists and Constructivists. All of these currents sought to redefine the relations between the critic or theorist and practical politics; and all of them could promote that project because of the political history to which they belonged. Students and academics who want to make a difference to the world may well feel frustrated that such a history is not, at the moment, ours; but they should not feel guilty about it. That such a history is not ours is largely the responsibility of our political antagonists.

Some years ago, I was associated with a worker writers' movement in Britain, and went down to Bristol to speak at a workshop of working-class men and women who were trying to write their life histories. I was speaking to them about the idea of autobiography, trying to keep my remarks as lucid as possible, when an almost-blind woman in her eighties interrupted me in her rich West Country burr to ask rather brusquely: "What kind of language is that you're talking?" I was just on the point of apologising for any unintentional obscurantism, and for being so remote from my audience, when she added: "Because I'd like to learn it". She went on to publish a magnificent history of her life, to which I added a brief introduction. There are, as the old cliché has it, times when it all seems worthwhile...

Chapter 2
Tales of Western Adventure

Patricia Limerick

I am sitting at a desk behind a name-plate that identifies me as "Dr Patricia Limerick, Marriage Counselor". I am looking earnestly and sincerely into a camera lens, and from time to time, an attentive person darts in to restore my make-up or tame my hair. I am undergoing repeated bouts of gratitude for the fact that I took improvisational theater in college. When the sound setting and the camera angle are right, I say my lines as sincerely and convincingly as I can: "I may not know your name, but I do know one pretty private thing about you. You have been involved in a tempestuous relationship, pursuing a mad romance . . . with fossil fuels". The Center of the American West is making a documentary, the first enterprise (that we have ever heard of!) to take literally the familiar metaphor of "America's love affair with petroleum", and put it to work to make a therapeutic case for moving on to a new, more lasting and gratifying relationship with energy efficiency and renewables.

On another occasion, I am sitting in an armchair on a stage. On my left (the audience's right) is John F. Kennedy's and Lyndon B. Johnson's Secretary of the Interior Stewart Udall. On my right (the audience's left) is Ronald Reagan's first Secretary of the Interior, James G. Watt. To many people engaged in environmental issues, Udall and Watt represent matter and anti-matter. The Center of the American West has brought them together in Boulder for two days, and the conversation between them has been intensely interesting, and chronically surprising.

Career-wise, improbability and adventure have become my norm. One collateral benefit of these wild activities is this: it is hard for me to remember why other academics choose to feel marginalized.

"Come on in, the water's fine!" I would like to say to graduate students and assistant professors. There is certainly plenty of room in this pool. In the early twenty-first century, there is no limit or constraint on the desire of public constituencies to profit from the perspective of a university-based historian. Even better, the usual lament of the humanities—"There is plenty of money to support work in science and engineering, but very little to support work in the humanities"—proves to be accurate only if you define "work in the humanities" in the narrowest and most conventional way. If "work in the humanities" means only individualistic research, directed at arcane topics detached from real-world needs and written in inaccessible and insular jargon, there is indeed very limited money. But for a humanities professor willing to take up applied work, funding sources are unexpectedly abundant. There is, for instance, no need for humanities professors to waste any more time in envying the resources available to scientists and engineers. Instead, you can offer to play Virgil to their Dante (though you might profitably skip this evocative, but not universally familiar way of describing your services), guiding them through the inferno of cultural anxieties, laypeople's misunderstandings, and political landmines.

Our "Virgilian guide service" at the University of Colorado operates under the more prosaic name of the Center of the American West. My co-founder, the distinguished law professor and very public scholar, Charles Wilkinson, and I created this entity in 1986. A great deal of improvisation and experimentation took place in the following decade and a half. When the dust settled, I had been transformed—from individualistic humanities professor primarily focused on my own academic work even while writing op-ed pieces and making occasional speeches to public audiences—into "faculty director and chair of the board of the Center of the American West". The Center had applied projects; the projects required the collaborative work of others, ranging from permanent staff members to graduate and undergraduate students; the employees expected to be paid; and this, in turn, caused me to expect to wake, periodically, at two in the morning, asking myself (1) how I had ended up with so many hostages to fortune crowded onto my little entrepreneurial vessel, and (2) how I was going to keep us all afloat.

We had very nice business cards, and on the back of our cards, we had this really quite accurate statement: "The Center of the American West takes as its mission the creation of forums for the respectful exchange of ideas and perspectives in the pursuit of solutions to the region's difficulties. We at the Center believe that an understanding of the historical origins of the West's problems, an emphasis on the common interests of all parties, and a dose of good humor are essential to constructive public discussion".

Twenty years after the Center's founding, we have put this mission statement into practice in projects aplenty.[1] The 1997 publication of *Atlas of the New West*, captained by my wonderful colleague in geography, Bill Travis, literally put us on the map with officials and citizens who are trying to assess and cope with change in the region. A series of lively, readable reports—on the boom/bust economy, on cleaning up abandoned mines, on energy efficiency and conservation—have positioned the Center as a credible, trustworthy supplier of worthwhile guidance on current problems. A nearly completed book on repair and restoration, *Healing the West*, brings together natural scientists, humanists, engineers, and social scientists who are engaged in finding remedies for dilemmas inherited from the region's past. Another nearly completed project, *The Nature of Justice: Racial Equity and Environmental Well-Being*, spotlights the political, cultural, and emotional involvement of ethnic minorities with outdoors environmental experience. We work regularly with federal agencies, ranging from the Environmental Protection Agency to the National Park Service. A generous pair of donors gave us an endowment that allows me to take undergraduates with me on outings; two students traveled with me to the Powder River Basin in Wyoming to mediate a session addressing the conflicts between ranchers who own the land's surface, and natural gas producers developing subsurface mineral rights, while another student traveled with me to MIT, teaming up with me on a presentation on the contradiction between the highly urbanized state of the West and its very rural image to the History Department. And perhaps most gratifying of all, we do K-12 teachers workshops.[2] Convention-bound professors are dedicated and gifted when it comes to lamenting and denouncing the lack of academic preparation evidenced in entering college students, making it a considerable pleasure to go beyond lamentation to working collaboratively with actual teachers.

In the most concrete, prosaic, down-to-earth, reliable way, the Center of the American West's work represents the realization of my dreams for higher education. In recent times, the Center has adopted the hopeful slogan, "Turning hindsight into foresight". Every time I use this slogan or see it in the Center's material, I receive a booster dosage of humility, an inoculation against overconfidence. Could it really be possible to turn hindsight into foresight? I believe we are obligated to try.

So why do I hold back on wholeheartedly and enthusiastically recruiting young colleagues into this wildly gratifying, intellectually invigorating territory?

- To conventional academics in the humanities, contact with the public, as well as the entrepreneurial pursuit of funding, registers as contamination and impurity.
- Effectiveness as a public scholar requires practices far more strenuous than the comfortable custom of reminding audiences of fellow academics, who are already sworn and certified fellow believers, of the virtue and validity of left-wing principles.
- The clarity of language necessary for reaching the public will, in the judgment of tradition-bound peer evaluators, convict its users of a lack of sophistication and a questionable level of expertise.
- The criteria used by academic humanities departments for hiring and promotion are half a century out of date, and yet they are persistent and powerful. By these standards, the work of a public

scholar can only register as service, a not-very-glorified act of volunteerism that will be counted as immeasurably inferior, as a demonstration of intellectual prowess, when compared with real research.

- While colleagues who feel recognized and validated for their own achievements will be the best of allies, professional jealousy and rivalry will radiate from the insecure. Those stricken with envy will circle around a successful public scholar like sharks around a lively, aquatic protein source. But there is good news: once tenure is in the bag, a preference for attacking from behind will keep these sharks from doing much damage. The fact that tenure serves primarily to protect the public scholar from her departmental colleagues is a little ironic, but the person who finds herself in need of this protection develops quite an enthusiastic taste for this particular irony.

Here is the upshot: to become a university-based public scholar, a young person may well have to put that ambition into cold storage for a decade and a half. Go to graduate school, write a conventional dissertation, get a tenure-track job, publish in academic journals and in university presses,[3] give papers at professional conferences to small groups of fellow specialists, comply with all the requirements of deference, conformity, and hoop jumping that narrow the road to tenure while also narrowing the travelers on that road, and *then* take up the applied work that appealed to you in the first place. You may need to write yourself a thorough and eloquent memo, early in this process, and store it in an easily remembered and retrievable place, to remind yourself of the postponed and mothballed ambition to connect with the world that got you psyched for this career in the first place.

I have my fingers crossed that I have this all wrong. I live with the hope that over the next couple of decades, I will receive letters and e-mails aplenty beginning:

> Dear Patty, I read your crabby list of bullet points and your gloomy predictions about the fifteen years needed before a young academic could become a public scholar. I am pleased to inform you that I have proven your predictions entirely wrong! Higher education turned out to be capable of much more rapid and searching change than you ever imagined, and I am about to tell you, using examples from my own career and that of many friends, how wrong you were!

In truth, at the University of Colorado, Boulder, the Faculty Council and the Faculty Affiliates of the Center of the American West add up to one big indication that my assessment may be wonderfully inaccurate. From civil engineering to religious studies, from linguistics to botany, from ethnomusicology to law, this university fields a magnificent team of faculty who refuse to be cloistered. And, in the same spirit, when I leave my campus and travel to conventions of professional historians, I find many professors from other campuses who are at work in all sorts of applied ways, serving as expert witnesses in litigation on behalf of Indian tribes, working closely with K-12 teachers, consulting with elected and appointed officials, providing perspective and direction to governmental agencies and advocacy groups.

But I still worry about the sustainability of higher education's current practices, especially in the rigid and anachronistic standards of evaluation that drive hiring and promotion. And I cannot shake the idea, composed of equal parts gloom and cheer, that the minds of faculty and students are the most under-utilized renewable resource in the United States today.

The barriers and obstacles to getting that resource unleashed and put to productive use are located—and surely this must be good news—in our own turf and in our own habits. Public receptivity to scholars who speak clearly, pragmatically, and originally is demonstrably unbounded. When we give up jargon and pontification, when we substitute humility for smugness, when we listen intensely and respectfully to people who have acquired their expertise in front-line practice, and maybe especially when we undertake to attend to and understand political positions that do not match our own, the barriers and obstacles that currently block the full engagement of professors with the public, dissolve. And there are now enough practitioners of public scholarship to serve as mentors, providing experience-tempered encouragement and guidance to aspirants and apprentices.

In the search for mentors, when I was a senior in college back in 1972, my roommate had a considerable advantage over me: she knew what she wanted to do, while I could not get my imagination to move past the disturbing fact that I would not remain a college student forever.

My roommate knew that she yearned to work in theater, but it was still no easy matter to transform this ambition into an actual job. She tried writing to stage managers around the country, asking for their help and advice. The last words of one particular letter, responding to her inquiry, caught our attention. "I am a fraud", this forthright, but self-disqualifying mentor confessed, "I cannot help you".

As 21-year-olds, we had heard the platitude, "The more you know, the more you realize what you do not know". So we knew where this fellow was coming from. We were struck by his humility and his honesty, and we hoped that we would remember his example when (much more likely, *if*) we turned out to be established professionals ourselves.

And then, a few days later, we examined the letter more carefully. The last sentence, it turned out, disclosed more in the way of unusual handwriting than unusual modesty. Properly decoded, his conclusion actually read, "I am *afraid* I cannot help you".

Both phrasings appear in my mind with some regularity these days. Try this yourself (actually, don't try this, without fair warning and some practice): stand before an audience of federal employees, environmental advocates, county commissioners, state legislators, utility managers, or urban and regional planners. Have these people look earnestly and expectantly at you, radiating the faith that a university-based historian will be able to say something that will be concretely and pragmatically useful to them in their lives and careers. Based on my own experience, I can promise that you will have a moment when you will feel as if the only honest thing to say is, "I am a fraud, and I am also afraid, because I cannot help you".

But don't say that.

The very good news is that there is no need to confess either to fraudulence or fear, since it is perfectly possible to cultivate the skills and strategies that allow us to deliver on the promise that university-based academics are of value to the world around us, in very direct ways. Here are several techniques I rely on every day:

- Study your audience as closely and attentively as you study your academic sources. Use every opportunity to demonstrate that you know who they are, that you respect the complexity and challenge of their lives, and that you have thought hard about what is the most useful information and knowledge to bring to them.
- Face up to the fact that your own opinions and convictions may not be the final word in human wisdom. With this recognition under your belt, you surrender the pomposity and pretension that can poison professorial efforts to communicate with the public.
- Apply, to the world around you, the methods they taught you in graduate school for assessing evidence. Take in information carefully and contemplatively; keep your hypotheses in a limber and flexible state; do not leap to conclusions; resist the common human habit of celebrating the evidence that supports your pre-existing point of view, while dismissing the evidence that invites you to question your initial assumptions.
- If you can find a way of making your case without angering your audience, getting their backs up, and making them defensive, by all means, choose that approach. Direct verbal combat is very fun and self-satisfying, and rarely very productive of conversion or change.
- When you are misunderstood or harshly criticized, thank your ostensible opponent for giving you this opportunity to deepen your understanding and to sharpen your thinking. This response has the advantage of turning sensible, good-natured adversaries into allies, while also making less sensible, ill-tempered adversaries look pretty darned bad.

- Dedicate yourself to having a good time in the company of the wider public, and to conveying a sense of vigor, a refusal of fatalism, and a profound gratitude for your audience's willingness to give you a hearing. Remember that you will not have the opportunity to give members of the public a mid-term or final; you do not have the power to coerce their attention or to give them a grade. You have only one resource to bank on, and that is their good will; good will is a wonderful gift from a public audience, but decidedly not a gift to take for granted.

Western American History offers an abundance of parables, delivering equal supplies of stories of inspiration and cautionary tales, and those parables have given the Center of the American West its principal asset and main stock in trade. And so, as eager as I am to recruit new travelers on this trail of adventure, I cannot escape Lansford Hastings. Hastings did not become a household name, but the people who took his advice and followed his guidance became very famous indeed. The faith that the Donner Party put in Hastings' *The Emigrant's Guide to Oregon and California* set them off on a torturous trail through the mountains and deserts of the Great Basin and led them to entrapment in the snows of the Sierra. Three months after being rescued, one survivor, the child Virginia Reed, wrote her cousin a letter with this unforgettable line: "Never take no cutofs and hury along as fast as you can" (Stewart 1960:287). Virginia's advice, at the very least, reminds us that the challenges and difficulties of the public scholar's life do not involve life and death. But the advice retains resonance for this much less mortal realm: in the current circumstances of higher education, young travelers would be wise to avoid "cut-offs" and to travel the prescribed route to tenure, while still hurrying along as fast as they can.

The nation and the planet need their help.

Endnotes

[1] Visit our website at http://www.centerwest.org.

[2] The Gilder Lehrman Institute for American History has an extraordinary track record in recruiting and sponsoring high-visibility academics in work with K-12 teachers.

[3] It is important to note that many university presses are reaching for wider audiences, and encouraging scholars to explore their work for wider implications.

Reference

Stewart G R (1960) *Ordeal by Hunger.* New York: Pocket Books, Simon & Schuster.

Chapter 3
Open Letter to C. Wright Mills

Michael Burawoy

Dear Mills,

Excuse the familiarity, but I've known you for a very long time. I first read *The Power Elite* (1956) in 1970 when I was preparing for my MA in social anthropology in Zambia. I then read it again in 1973 while studying for my sociology PhD at the University of Chicago. You should know that this unmasking of the concentration of power has become a classic text, a mainstay in any political sociology class. It has enduring truth—the interlocking of corporate, military and political elites making life and death decisions that affect us all.

I read your *White Collar* (1951) and *New Men of Power* (1948) while I was writing my dissertation that was an ethnography of industrial work. *White Collar* long anticipated the 1970s interest in the transformation of work and the new middle class, while *New Men of Power* spoke to the cynicism with which rank and file workers regard their labor leaders. Both retain powerful insights for the world of today. I can't remember when I first read *The Sociological Imagination* (1959), but I think it must have been in Zambia too—the appendix on the sociologist as "craftsman" was inspiring and comforting in those lonely days when I wondered whether I'd ever make it as a sociologist. It has roused generations of sociologists to engage the big issues of the day. Reading it has become an initiation rite for graduate students.

In recent years I have had reason to return to *The Sociological Imagination* because there you gesture toward the idea of "public sociology"—the sociologist talking to publics and at kings. You would be amused to know that the idea of public sociology is enjoying quite a little renaissance in this country, especially following the meetings of the American Sociological Association in 2004, which were devoted to public sociology. I'm sure you would have difficulty believing that the sociology profession would be so interested in public sociology, and perhaps you would be even more surprised to learn that such a meeting would break all records of attendance and involvement! There was a hum and buzz about the possibilities of public sociologies. I'm sure you would have had your criticisms, but still you should be pleased at what you have inspired from so many years ago.

You would have appreciated the electrifying panel on W.E.B. Du Bois, even though I don't think you ever refer to his writings, and the address on the sociology of human rights from Mary Robinson, former President of Ireland and High Commissioner for Human Rights at the UN. The high point, however, was surely Arundhati Roy's oration on "Public Power in the Age of Globalization". She did not mince her words about US Imperialism. The conference ended with the massively attended debate about the fate of neoliberalism—the return to market fundamentalism that you, like so many others, thought was relegated to the past. The protagonists in the debate were two major public figures— one a sociologist and two-time President of Brazil, Fernando Henrique Cardoso, and the other an economist and acerbic columnist for *The New York Times*, Paul Krugman.

The issues we debated in San Francisco in 2004 were not that different from the ones that pre-occupied you in the 1950s. Sociology has moved on from what it was in your day, in part because of the legacy you left us, in part because social movements shattered the consensus sociology of the 1950s. Mainstream sociology is no longer so euphoric about the United States as the "exceptional" society, a paragon of truth and beauty. As you told us 50 years ago, if the US "leads" it does so by force of arms rather than force of ideas or of example. Power and inequality have become central to the sociological agenda, which has assumed a more global focus, although we still have a long way to go in provincializing our sociology, that is, recognizing how spurious are so many of its claims to universalism. Today sociologists devote a lot of attention to dominations, exclusions and marginality along lines of race, gender and even sexuality—issues that are entirely foreign to your writings, notwithstanding occasional flashes of redemption.

Public sociology has become the focus of many recent debates in professional journals in the United States, but also in countries as different as South Africa, Finland, China, Hungary, France, Russia, Portugal, Brazil, Germany, and England. In the last year three books have appeared, devoted to the issues raised by public sociology. The concern with public engagement can also be found in neighboring disciplines such as anthropology and geography. So it seems to have become almost a little social movement. This is not so surprising when one considers that most of us became sociologists out of dissatisfaction with the world around us, and believe me, today, there is a lot to be dissatisfied with.

I teach sociology at Berkeley, and have done so since 1977. It is a university that came of age in the 1950s with the explosion of higher education. It housed the leading department of sociology in the late 1950s and early 1960s, when you had already turned your back on the profession. Indeed, Berkeley's sociological star would rise until the explosion of the Free Speech Movement in 1964—students rising up against the suffocating society you so vividly portray in *White Collar* and *The Power Elite*. Indeed, many trace the student movement that spread across the country and indeed even the world, to your own writings. One of the major student leaders, Tom Hayden, devoted his MA to your work. It was written in the early 1960s, but only recently published as *Radical Nomad*. Following the Free Speech Movement the Berkeley Sociology Department was drowned in conflict for two decades. When it reemerged in the 1990s it did so with its commitment to public engagement intact.

This semester I have had the rare privilege of teaching an undergraduate seminar on contemporary theory. We devoted ourselves to your work, fathoming your notion of public sociology. We, therefore, began with *The Sociological Imagination*, interrogating its every page to work out the project you lay out. The idea was to see whether and how you followed this project in your own treatises on US society. But first we set the theoretical scene with readings from Thorstein Veblen's *The Theory of the Leisure Class* to which I believe you are heavily indebted, despite all those combative remarks in *The Power Elite*. We even read the reviled Talcott Parsons. I think students were inclined to sympathize with the mockery you made of his work. Then we took a taste of the great Robert Merton, your sponsor and supporter for so long, sadly neglected today. I believe he had a major influence on your early career. The remainder of the course was devoted to *The New Men of Power*, *White Collar*, *The Power Elite* and *Listen, Yankee*. We discovered that each book in your trilogy could be divided into two—sociological analysis and political program. So we discussed each book in two installments—in the first we compared your frame with the classics and in the second we compared your analysis with the world today.

Let me give you a sense of what sociology students of today read so that you can better appreciate our criticisms. They had already taken two semesters of classical social theory. In the first semester they learned Marxism as an evolving intellectual and political tradition. We started with Adam Smith before moving on to Marx and Engels and from there to Lenin, Gramsci and finally to Fanon. My assumption is that sociology cannot exist without its sparring partner, Marxism! I know your last book was your own version of the Marxist tradition but, sad to say, you gave only passing mention to the writings of the Italian Marxist Antonio Gramsci (1891–1937). His notions of hegemony and civil society give a very different frame for understanding US society and, indeed, public sociology. We'll come back to that! I'm even sadder that you did not get to read Frantz Fanon. His book *The Wretched of the Earth*, first published in 1961, became the bible for revolutionary change in Africa and the Third World more generally, and indeed it was also adopted by black revolutionaries in the United States during the 1960s. Many of Fanon's arguments are similar to those you yourself made about the

Cuban Revolution in *Listen, Yankee*, although he writes as a participant in the anti-colonial war of Algeria.

Anyway, students are well schooled in Marxism when they come to Durkheim and Weber in the second semester. You don't have much to say about Durkheim but your selection of writings from Max Weber—the one you undertook with Hans Gerth—has lived on as perhaps the definitive collection of Weber's writings. Again we are enormously in debt to you for providing an alternative Weber to the one proposed by your nemesis, Talcott Parsons. You'll be interested to know that after Weber we read a very different type of theorist, a Frenchman by the name of Michel Foucault, a theorist of power and postmodernity—a notion you already prefigured in *The Sociological Imagination*—whose fame has spread across the world. He's a bit obsessed with power, just as Durkheim is obsessed with solidarity. Indeed, he is Durkheim's Other. There's an uncanny correspondence between Durkheim's mechanical and organic solidarities and Foucault's sovereign and disciplinary powers. His ideas of disciplinary power or biopower are akin to those of rationalization in Weber. Foucault offers altogether different approaches to your mass society, which he would regard as the product of insidious micro-powers. The metaphor for contemporary society is the prison! How do you like that!

Finally, we turn to the modern history of feminism. This is an area of social thought quite beyond your ken. Students were appalled by your condescending characterization of women in *White Collar*, especially the sections on "the salesgirls" and "the white-collar girl". I was surprised you so completely missed the boat on gender since your hero Thorstein Veblen was such an ardent feminist and spoke about the exploitation of women in a consumer culture with such vitriol. No matter. We start with Simone De Beauvoir's *The Second Sex*, which first appeared in French in 1949. Just as you inspired but did not anticipate the student movement so De Beauvoir unknowingly laid the foundation of a feminist movement she could not imagine. We then read two texts of what we now call second wave feminism of the 1970s and 1980s: Catharine MacKinnon, a radical feminist, and Patricia Hill Collins, a more conciliatory feminist who insists on the intersection of gender with race and class. I tell you all this so that you can better understand how we reacted to your own work.

As I said, we began with *The Sociological Imagination*, which seemed to be a settling of accounts with sociology, published in 1959 only three years before you died. The notion that the sociological imagination is a quality of mind that turns personal troubles into public issues is perhaps the most oft-repeated mantra of the sociologist's self-representation. It is, indeed, a powerful idea. You might even say that it captures the project of public sociology. But we detected an unwarranted slippage across the line from, on the one side, the linking of *social milieu to social structure*, showing how our daily lives are shaped by forces beyond our immediate control, to, on the other side, turning *personal troubles into public issues*, which is a political project.

On one side of the line, sociologists demonstrate that the individual's experience is not a product of individual idiosyncrasy but of social forces. People commit suicide, says Durkheim, not only from an inner impulse but also because of an external compulsion, specifically, the state of society, egoistic, anomic, altruistic. Capitalism was born, says Weber, because of the unintended consequences of the Protestant Ethic. Calvinists thought they were serving God but they were actually creating the enormous fateful cosmos of modern rational capitalism! The capitalist system, Marx avers, is brought down by capitalists competing with one another for profit, inventing new ways to extract surplus from their workers. As they conscientiously pursue their daily surplus, they know not what they do, destroying the foundations of their very existence. As you know in the United States people explain their descent into poverty as bad luck or inadequate application but sociologists know better—they claim that poverty and unemployment are a product of the nature of the capitalist economy. Responding to Herrnstein and Murray's now famous *The Bell Curve*, which argues that inequality springs from the inevitably unequal distribution of individual intelligence, Berkeley sociologists wrote *Inequality By Design*, focusing on the institutions that produce social and economic inequality. These are just a few ways in which we illustrate your idea of the sociological imagination.

So far so good. But recognizing the link between social milieu and social structure does not mean crossing the line, turning personal troubles into public issues. Knowing that my unease or malaise is due to anomie in society, or knowing that I'm without a job because I live in a world of unregulated capitalism does not necessarily lead me to turn my personal trouble into a public issue. In fact, knowing the power of social structures is just as likely to paralyze as to mobilize. Indeed, sociological insight may even be universal but that would not guarantee bringing personal troubles into the public sphere. This is your first scholastic fallacy— that knowledge is liberating. Today, following Michel Foucault, we are more likely to follow the bleak hypothesis that sociological knowledge is disabling, incapacitating, a form of control. I know you saw that sociology could be used to serve power, as in your article "A Marx for managers", but you thought that if sociologists were independent then their sociological imagination was liberating. Not necessarily so.

But let us not descend into postmodern pessimism. Understanding the relation between milieu and structure may not be liberating in itself, but it still may be necessary for such liberation. In addition to sociological imagination we also need a *political imagination*. Your books, actually, make this very clear, and most interesting, your political imagination shifts over time. In *New Men of Power* you offer a bold criticism of labor leaders who had lost touch with their members as they reached for the power elite. Rank and file workers are marooned by the status anxiety of their labor leaders in their relation to their negotiating partners from corporate capital, or by the temptations of racketeering with local contractors. That's the sociological imagination. But you end the book where you begin, with a variety of publics—Far Left, Independent Left, Liberal Center, Practical Right and Sophisticated Right—that are active in relation to the question of labor. They have detached themselves from the mass society of inert publics—the underdogs, the working class and the middle class. You propose a socialist political program that calls for a labor party, worker control of production and democratic planning. This is a radical program, indeed, reflecting the radicalism of the left publics, and intended to bring the working class from inertness to alertness—a public in itself to a public for itself! But this program remained abstract. It would have to contend with the shock troops of the "practical right" and, then as back-up, the material concessions and ideological weapons of the "sophisticated right".

As you quickly learned, the balance of forces was never favorable to such a radical program—your political imagination was utopian. Whether it was because the anticipated slump and ensuing political crisis never materialized, or because inertness is far more deeply implanted than you recognized, your political imagination could not connect personal troubles to public issues. Things haven't got better since! Indeed, there has been a steady decline in organized labor since the 1950s. Today only 7.4% of the labor force in the private sector is unionized, as compared to a peak of 36% in your day. If there is any bright spot it is organizing in the service sector, organizing of immigrants, and the importance of appealing to identities beyond simply working class. Your analysis of the breaking of ties between leaders and led prefigured the demise of the labor movement.

In your next book, *White Collar*, your political imagination takes a more cautious turn. But first let me congratulate you on this brilliant sociological analysis of the demise of the old middle classes (small entrepreneurs) and the rise of the new middle classes (the new professions, the sales workers, and the expansion of the office). It's a *tour de force*, bringing together Weber's analysis of bureaucratization and Marx's analysis of class. You anticipate so much that came after you and for which you have not been given enough credit, for example studies of deskilling, pioneered by Harry Braverman's *Labor and Monopoly Capital* (1974), that became an industry in the 1970s, or your idea of the sale of personality in service work that Arlie Hochschild's *Managed Heart* (1983) would term emotional labor. Once again you show the link between social milieu and social structure, how white collar workers' sense of unease and alienation is caused by the broader anonymous forces of corporate capitalism or what you call the main drift.

There's no shortage of sociological imagination here, but what has happened to your political imagination? You end up arguing that the middle classes find themselves in what Erik Olin Wright called "contradictory class locations". They waver between the dominant and subordinate classes; they are no vanguard, they are the rearguard, flowing with political winds, and in your time the winds came from the main drift of corporate capitalism. There was no sign that personal troubles would turn into public issues. That hasn't changed, even though in recent years we have seen a systematic assault on the new middle classes with downsizing, outsourcing, overwork and deskilling within corporations. Again your analysis prefigured so much, except you gave the impression of a stagnant monopoly capitalism whereas it has proved most dynamic under the pressure of competition, especially from foreign capital.

The final book in the trilogy, *The Power Elite*, curiously created much less excitement among today's students than the previous two. While this was indeed another bold move to be making in 1956, especially in view of reigning paradigms of pluralism—the idea of the power elite has been broadly assimilated into the collective consciousness of the United States. Again, knowing that one's life is so profoundly controlled by interlocking corporate, military and political elites is as likely to lead to cynicism and apathy rather than anger and action. Notwithstanding your own anger at the higher immorality, I think you were also skeptical that corporate exploitation could mobilize public sentiment. At the end of the book you juxtapose your mass society, seduced by consumerism, indoctrinated by the media, distracted by celebrities, to a democratic republic in which publics express their views openly, debate with one another, have their expressed needs realized under the assumption that this public sphere is autonomous from dominant institutions such as state and economy. This is harking back to a bygone period of Jeffersonian democracy rather than pointing forward to new possibilities. This retreat into an imagined past suggested that you had given up on the project of turning personal troubles into public issues, even before you announced it in *The Sociological Imagination*!

What we didn't like about *The Power Elite* was your characterization of mass society, which missed the contestations that do arise and, of course, did arise soon after you died—the student movement, the women's movement, the civil rights movement, the anti-war movement. I'm sure you'd be surprised to learn about all these, since *The Power Elite* intimated no opposition from below. To be quite honest, we have been more persuaded by Gramsci's theory of hegemony than your theory of manipulation. Instead of an incoherent mass society, we think of civil society made up of organizations, movements, and publics. Instead of mass deception and false consciousness, we believe that subaltern groups do have a good sense within their common sense, and that they actively consent to domination. This is not a matter of false consciousness—consent is rational and it can be withdrawn. From this Gramscian standpoint it is far easier to understand the appearance of the movements of the 1960s and 1970s.

We must now return to *The Sociological Imagination*. In the chapter on politics you distinguish the "independent intellectual"—your model for yourself—from the Philosopher King, the intellectual who rules in the name of superior knowledge, and the advisor to the King, the servant of power. You fear that the servants of power, the technicians, the experts, are taking over our discipline. They accept the terms of their clients, solve their problems and receive their paychecks. Your fears were exaggerated. Today the world of power, whether corporations or states, is less enthusiastic about sociology—perhaps because you were so successful in giving it a radical color! And so, whether we like it or not, our political role concerns talking to publics and at kings.

But how should we talk to publics? Your modus operandi, I have to tell you this, is to talk down to publics. You place yourself above publics. In fact you don't believe there really are any publics except the New York intellectuals that surround you. For the rest you have mass society, atomized, deceived, and manipulated individuals. It's as if making direct contact with people would contaminate you or your thoughts. There is a deep elitism in your detachment. You represent what I would call *traditional public sociology*—books written for but not with publics.

There is another type of public sociology, what I call *organic public sociology*, in which the sociologist steps out of the protected environment of the academy and reaches into the pockets of civil society. The organic public sociologist enters into an unmediated dialogue with neighborhood associations, with communities of faith, with labor movements, with prisoners. If, for traditional public sociology, publics, say the readership of *The New York Times*, are national, thin (people hardly aware of one another), passive, and mainstream, the organic publics are likely to be local, thick, active and often counter-publics.

It's a pity you did not live to see the feminist movement take root, because it represented an impressive case of organic public sociology. As Catharine MacKinnon once wrote, "Feminism is the first theory to emerge from those whose interests it affirms". Feminism didn't only connect social milieu to social structure but also turned personal troubles into public issues, as when wife beating became the felony of battery, as when sexual harassment and rape became subject to legal proceedings. Suddenly, as the feminists said, the personal became political and the rule of men was recognized as political regulation. Women were no longer chattel. You missed out on Simone De Beauvoir's *The Second Sex*, an amazing grand historical analysis of the social, political, economic and cultural forces that have conspired to maintain male hegemony with the complicity of women. Patricia Hill Collins, writing in the 1980s, brought race and class to radical feminism, arguing that those suffering from multiple forms of subjugation have the greatest insight into the social structures that oppress them. No shortage of sociological imagination among African–American women, expressed in tales, narratives and songs. The lesson: even the devastated ghettos of our nation are no mass society of deceived and ignorant people who need to have their understanding brought to them from the all-knowing sociologist. African–American women possess a common sense with a kernel of good sense, that is a good measure of sociological imagination, which they express in their cultural forms and, albeit more rarely, in social movements. Black feminists have borrowed from, entered into a dialogue with, elaborated and articulated what is often taken for granted by their sisters.

When they act as organic public sociologists, black feminists do not immerse themselves in their communities but instead retain a measure of independence that allows them a distinctive standpoint from which to enter a dialogue with those communities. They are after all still sociologists, but they are not your craft worker, insulated from the rest of professional sociology. As Collins makes clear, here too, there is dialogue between the African–American woman and the hegemonic forms of sociology, trying to shift the latter in a more humane and universalistic direction. No less than in your idealization of the independent intellectual, so in your characterization of the sociologist as craftworker you suffer, if I may be so bold as to say so, from a blunted sociological imagination. You commit the second scholastic fallacy, one you share with those pure scientists, the high priests of objectivity that you calumniated. You seem to believe that the purest and truest ideas somehow emerge tabula rasa from the mind of the intellectual and that partaking in society is a contamination. Engagement, you imply, must be at a distance.

Yes, I know you faced a hostile and uncomprehending world of triumphalist sociology, but still you were part of a common disciplinary division of labor that is here to stay. You can't retreat back into a world of the autonomous intellectual, a world that no longer exists. We are living in a very different time from Marx, Durkheim and Weber, we are living in a world of developed social science disciplines in which the craftworker has become an anachronism. We have to move forward to a division of sociological labor in which we learn from one another without sacrificing our independence.

Professional sociology will suffer from the pathologies you so brilliantly describe in *The Sociological Imagination*—the grand theory of Talcott Parsons removed from the concrete world, and the abstracted empiricism of Paul Lazarsfeld that has lost touch with any context whether theoretical or societal—if it loses touch with the very sort of public sociology you and others represent. Today, the aim of critical sociologists, like yourself, must not be to destroy professional sociology but to bring it into dialogue with public sociology. As a work of critical sociology, *The Sociological Imagination* pointed in two directions: on the one hand toward a public sociology, and on the other hand, against the foundations of professional sociology, whether those foundations be value foundations or theoretical and methodological assumptions. Just as professional sociology supplies the tools for a policy sociology, geared to solve the problems of clients, so critical sociology not only targets professional sociology, but also infuses values into our public debates and engagements.

What values does sociology represent? In *The Sociological Imagination* you are quite explicit that the ultimate values upon which both sociology and society rest are those of reason and freedom. Without doubt those values are important, but are they the values that distinguish sociology from other sciences? In referring to freedom and reason you perhaps reflected the threats to those values from fascism and communism. Today, I might suggest that the values that underpin sociology are justice and equality—very much the continuing legacy of the transformation of sociology in the 1960s and 1970s.

Let me come to the end of my overly long letter. My admiration for your work knows no bounds. Your place in the history of sociology is assured. You have rightly been rediscovered as a pioneer of public sociology. But your vision here is still stuck in the past. Harking back to the classics of the nineteenth century and upholding the mythology of the non-attached free-floating intellectual, you present us with the Janus faced sociologist—facing outwards is the independent intellectual talking down to publics and at kings, facing inwards is the self-absorbed craftworker, fighting off the pathologies of professionalization.

Today we replace your individual monad with a division of sociological labor—a matrix of professional, policy, critical and public sociologies in which the flourishing of each is dependent upon the flourishing of all, a matrix which aims for an organic interdependence, and, at least in the United States, struggles against the hegemony of professional and policy sociology. In Marx, Weber, and Durkheim these four types of sociology combine seamlessly, but today they are separate types of interdependent knowledge, each with its own distinctive notions of truth, legitimacy, accountability, power and pathology. As individuals we tend to specialize in one or more of these four types of knowledge, sometimes moving between them, but hopefully never forgetting the joint project that unites us—to create a more humane, equal and just society. To do this a sociological imagination will not be enough, we will also need a political imagination.

From your long time admirer,

Michael Burawoy, May 2007

References

Braverman H (1974) *Labor and Monopoly Capital*. New York: Monthly Review Press.
De Beauvoir S (1962 [1949]) *The Second Sex*. New York: Alfred A. Knopf.
Fanon F (1961) *The Wretched of the Earth*. New York: Grove Press.
Gerth H and Wright Mills C (1942) A Marx for Managers. *Ethics: An International Journal of Legal, Political and Social Thought* 52(2):200–215.
Hayden T *Radical Nomad*. Boulder, CO: Paradigm.
Hochschild A *Managed Heart*. Berkeley: University of California Press.
Wright Mills C (1948) *New Men of Power.* New York: Harcourt Brace.
Wright Mills C (1951) *White Collar.* New York: Oxford University Press.
Wright Mills C (1956) *The Power Elite.* New York: Oxford University Press.
Wright Mills C (1959) *The Sociological Imagination.* New York: Oxford University Press.
Wright Mills C (1960) *Listen, Yankee*. New York: Ballantine.
Veblen T (1899) *The Theory of the Leisure Class*. New York: The MacMillan Company.

Chapter 4

Craven Emotional Warriors

Melissa W. Wright

Plan B

I and many people with whom I work have, once again, been called "ideological crackpots". I was just sitting down to work on this essay when I decided to peruse the local daily and see what was happening in the opinion pages, only to discover that another right-wing editorialist is taking cheap shots at scholars in women's studies, in addition to those in ethnic studies and comparative literature, for being, as he writes, "craven emotional warriors" (Rodriguez 2007). In other words, we're all crazy, and hormonal. We have heard this before.

I shot off an email to the *Los Angeles Times*-based author; sent a short note to the women's studies list, and will soon consult with colleagues about whether we should craft a public response. All before finishing my morning cup of tea, and all in a day's work in women's studies. I am also in the geography department, but we geographers do not deal with these kinds of editorials on a regular basis. I can't think of one that has questioned the legitimacy of the discipline and our scholarship *tout court*. But women's studies departments—our scholarship, our classes, and even just our professional existence as feminists—are constantly a matter of public debate. We are always, already "public" scholars. And so are our students who, when they choose to major in women's studies, receive an immediate education in the politicization of knowledge as they must constantly explain and defend their academic choices.

And particularly in Pennsylvania, where the state legislature set up a committee to examine "bias" in the state education system, women's studies departments in the state university system have been much discussed in legislative committee sessions. My class, "global feminisms," was declared, among many other apparently "radical" courses, "corrupt" on a right-wing watchdog website, and the department head of women's studies (Lorraine Dowler), also another geographer, now has numerous skills for dealing with public debate over women's studies curricula and pedagogy. There is no ivory tower for this department. We were never invited in the first place and, well, the public just won't let us go climb up. So we're here in the trenches of public education, public funding and public accountability.

But I hadn't planned to write about women's studies departments in this essay as I was all set to write about a social justice movement in northern Mexico. Yet, there is undeniably a connection to what I had intended to write, and if my experience as a feminist scholar with an appointment in women's studies means anything, illustrating such connections is one of the challenges facing public scholars around the world. And so now I return to Plan A.

Plan A

Since the mid-1990s, protests in northern Mexico have brought international attention to the violence that, for more than a decade, has claimed hundreds of women's lives along the Mexico–US border. Activists and scholars have called this violence, "femicide", in reference not only to the crimes but to the impunity that surrounds them (Monárrez Fragoso 2001). The anti-femicide protests consist of diverse domestic and international organizations and individuals who demand that the Mexican government implement strategies for preventing further violence and that it convict those responsible for the crimes. But far from being simple, these demands have provoked a high-stakes controversy over the meaning of women's activism in public space. For, as the protestors take to the streets and demand justice, they constantly encounter the accusation that they are violating the boundaries separating pure family women from those sullied by public ambitions. Within this distinction, the former represent upstanding members of society and the latter, social pariahs.

To understand the power of this accusation and its corrosive impact on the movement, we must investigate its underlying logic, which takes us to the conceptual distinction separating "public" and "private" women as if they were binary opposites (see Landes 1998). In Mexico, as in many places throughout the world, the concept of "public woman" evokes that of a woman whose moral character and actual physical body have been tarnished via her public activities (economic, political, and social). In Mexico, as elsewhere, the term, public woman ("la mujer pública") is most often represented in the negative image of the "prostitute", who stands for a contaminated woman who, by extension, contaminates her family, her community, and her nation (Castillo 1999). Meanwhile, "public man" ("el hombre público") is another way of saying "citizen".[1] By contrast, private women are the mothers, daughters, sisters and wives of the patriarchal family whose moral and corporeal integrity is protected by their domesticity. In dominant discourses within western liberal democracies, private women represent the good moral forces in society as opposed to the immoral public ones.

The public woman accusation first emerged around the anti-femicide protests in the mid-1990s when governing elites referred to the victims as "public women", or as women who acted like "whores" in manner and clothing (Tabuenca Córdoba 2003). With such references, the elites evoked the age-old blame-the-victim strategies still so common around the world for dismissing violence against women as provoked by the women themselves. Then, toward the end of the decade, they deployed the discourse as a strategy for dismissing the activists as "public women" whose radical political and economic agendas threatened the social fabric (Martínez Coronado 2003; Meza Rivera 2003). So, whereas political and corporate leaders have used the public women rhetoric to question the victims' morality, and, by extension, their innocence as "victims", they have used this same discourse against the activists as a means for challenging the activists' moral standing as "citizens". In this case, the elites charge that the activists are radical "feminists" who via their public activities are forsaking the family and the social institutions upon which it rests. Thus, by referring to the activists as feminists, and sometimes either explicitly or implicitly as lesbians, the governing elite has sought to turn public opinion against the anti-femicide movement by characterizing its leading activists as crazy extremists,[2] or one could say "ideological crackpots", who breed immorality.

The vitriol of these attacks over the years has successfully forced a restructuring of the ant-femicide movement away from feminist issues. Through the 1990s, the anti-femicide movement was spearheaded jointly by a coalition of women-run organizations along with victims' families to demand justice. With several Mexican feminists in the leading roles, they called for legislative changes to domestic violence and rape legislation and brought attention to the issues of gender equity at work as well as within the home. But by the late 1990s, the vilification of the feminist leaders played out in the local newspapers, and the coalition of women's organizations dissolved. The public woman discourse was front and center in these assaults as the accusations included claims that the feminists were "prostituting" the victims' families by "selling" their stories to an international public always eager for sensationalist accounts of sex and violence along the border (Guerrero and Minjáres 2004; Piñon Balderrama 2003).

And these attacks quickly took a toll on the movement as some organizations in the anti-femicide campaign publicly dissociated fully from "feminists" as a means for proving that their integrity as "real" private women who were not under the influence of the public, feminist ones. As a result, the coalitions within the movement have fragmented around the public–private women divide as some groups identify themselves as consisting of "domestic" women, or those who represent victims' families, as opposed to those consisting of "public" women, or those who advocate for women's rights more broadly.[3] Under such circumstances, the feminist/activist/academics, who have long been active in this movement, have faced tough choices between toning down their feminism or exposing themselves and the movement, more generally, to attack. By 2005, even though the feminist activists were spearheading important projects related to women's rights, violence against women and human rights, in addition to other issues,[4] they were no longer the visible leaders of the anti-femicide campaigns in northern Mexico. Meanwhile, controversies over the meaning of "public women" for the cause continue to weaken the remaining anti-femicide groups in which the accusation of being a feminist or merely associating with feminist activists leaves one vulnerable to being attacked as a "public woman".

So, as a feminist/activist/academic, I, among many others, have struggled with what it means to be a public scholar in this situation. The questions I contemplate are: how can feminist activists within this movement fight the public woman discourse without contributing to the divisions that weaken the movement's coalitions? What are the implications of the "public woman" for Mexican democracy, for women's participation in it, and for social justice movements worldwide? How can we strategize against the many ways for silencing women who speak in public and who are attacked as "crazy" or otherwise "not normal" simply by virtue of drawing attention to women's issues?[5] Such, and other related, questions arise against the obvious pressing need for more combined efforts between scholars and activists, and between scholarship and activism, across the binational border region (see Monárrez Fragoso and Tabuenca Córdoba 2008).

A, B . . .

These questions clearly reach far beyond the context of northern Mexico and the violence afflicting the border region. As the United Nations recently reported, violence against women represents one of the most serious problems facing humanity at a global scale, and yet, as this same report shows, for women, in particular, to fight against it is demonized as "perverse" around the world.[6] As Bob Herbert of *The New York Times* wrote, "We're all implicated in this carnage because the relentless violence against women and girls is linked at its core to the wider society's casual willingness to dehumanize women and girls, to see them first and foremost as sexual vessels—objects—and never, ever as the equals of men". So, why given the enormous magnitude of violence against women and the many problems it raises for public health and human well-being around the world, is fighting this violence, or even speaking about it, so controversial? Why are the women who do so called "ideological crackpots" or "*locas*"?

In contemplating such questions, we can see how the *Los Angeles Times* editorialist shares much in common with those wishing to silence the anti-femicide protests in northern Mexico. Both he and those who attack the anti-femicide activists declare feminists, among other scholars who question social privilege, to be public liabilities. Accordingly, the editorialist wants feminists tossed out of the academy for being "emotionally craven warriors" just as the elites in Mexico want feminists kept off the street and excluded from the democratic process for being "immoral" social influences. Fighting against such people, and the power they represent, is part and parcel of the work of feminism that shows how the binary separating public from private life, including public from private subjects, has long been a ploy for denying women access to power, resources and social justice. It is a struggle shared by women the world over who publicly express their opinions, who defy patriarchal control, who assert their independence over their bodies, who fight for women's access to resources and who demand justice by women and for women. And part of this fight includes constantly reworking the strategies for fighting a malicious discourse of "public women" that, like a loaded weapon, can be pointed at any woman, at any time, and in any place when she dares to make herself seen and heard in the public sphere. For this reason, feminists have no choice but to be "public scholars" in a world where to speak of women and for women is, more often than not, politically controversial.

Consequently, an essential part of feminist work also includes putting feminist arguments into the public media where, as recent studies have shown, women "are barely present in the faces seen, the voices heard and the opinions expressed in the world's media" (Pritchard 2006). The problem is not merely that women appear in the media as "experts" much less often than men; the problem is that women *hardly appear as experts at all*. According to a comprehensive global study of women's representation in the media as "experts" and as "spokespeople", women represent the former only 17% of the time and the latter even less (Gallagher 2005, Executive Summary).[7] So, as feminists craft responses to the "ideological-crackpot" editorialists and others of their ilk, we know that our chances of being published as "'out'" feminists are low, especially in the current climate where it is possible for an editorial writer for a major news chain, such as the *Los Angeles Times*, to attack scholars without engaging with their scholarship. And that's why we must keep writing as experts in action with women who dare to go public.

Endnotes

[1] I would like to thank Socorro Tabuenca for pointing out this linguistic distinction to me. I would also like to thank Joan Landes and Lorraine Dowler for their comments on this essay.

[2] Personal communication with Esther Chávez, Ciudad Juarez (2002).

[3] For instance, in a letter posted on the internet, Nuestras Hijas de Regreso a Casa, an organization of victims' family members and their supporters, broke ranks with the feminists who had organized the V-Day protest in Ciudad Juarez in February 2004. The letter

was posted on 17 January 2004 on http://amsterdam.nettime.org/Lists-Archives/nettime-1-0401/msg00055.html. I downloaded it on 26 January 2007 at 12:10 pm EST. The English translation is original to the document.

[4] An abbreviated list of organizations active in the anti-femicide and related campaigns in northern Mexico include the following: Amigos de las Mujeres de Juarez (http://www.amigosdemujeres.org/), which is a non-profit organization that has helped the victims' families by providing emotional and financial support to their groups through fundraising efforts, donations, and outreach. Casa Amiga: Centro de Crisis (http://www.casa-amiga.org/), a sexual assault, domestic violence and rape crisis center in Ciudad Juarez. Centro de Derechos Humanos de la Mujer (CDHM), a women's rights and human rights organization based in Chihuahua City that provides legal and communal support for victims of violence. Nuestras Hijas de Regreso a Casa (http://www.mujeresdejuarez.org/), an organization of family members and their supporters in Ciudad Juárez that has been active in organizing anti-femicide protests within Mexico and internationally. Justicia Para Nuestras Hijas (http://espanol.geocities.com/justhijas/#quienes), an organization of family members and their supporters in Chihuahua City that has been active in organizing protests within Mexico and internationally.

[5] In such instances, people who want to silence women call them "lesbian" as a means for characterizing them as abnormal and perverse women.

[6] For the UN report on violence against women, see http://daccessdds.un.org/doc/UNDOC/GEN/N06/419/74/PDF/N0641974.pdf

[7] The full report was authored by Gallagher (2005) as part of the World Association for Christian Communication and its Global Media Monitoring Project, conducted by a consortium of researchers around the world.

References

Castillo D (1999) Border lives: Prostitute women in Tijuana. *Signs* 24:387–433.

Gallagher M (2005) The Global Media Monitoring Project 2005, http://www.whomakesthenews.org/who_makes_the_news/report_2005 Accessed 16 December 2007.

Guerrero C and Minjáres G (2004) Hacen Mito y Lucro de Los Femincidios. *El Diario de Ciudad Juárez* 22 July:1A.

Landes J (ed) (1998) *Feminism, the Public and the Private*. Oxford: Oxford University Press.

Martínez Coronado B. (2003) Desintegración sociofamiliar, germen de crímenes: Patricio. *El Heraldo de Chihuahua* 20 February:1A.

Meza Rivera F (2003) Sí Reciben Donativos las ONGs. *El Heraldo de Chihuahua* 25 February:2, 25.

Monárrez Fragoso J (2001) Femincidio Sexual Serial en Ciudad Juárez: 1993–2001. *Debate Feminista* 25:279–308 (also available as Serial Sexual Femicide in Ciudad Juárez: 1993–2001, http://www.womenontheborder.org/articles Accessed 16 December 2007.

Monárrez Fragoso J and Tabuenca Córdoba M S (2008) *Bordeando la Violencia Contra las Mujeres en la Frontera Norte de México*. Tijuana: El Colegio de la Frontera Norte.

Piñon Balderrama D (2003) Lucran ONGs con Muertas. *El Heraldo de Chihuahua* 23 February:1A.

Pritchard S (2006) The media's missing women. *The Guardian Unlimited* 19 February. http://observer.guardian.co.uk/readerseditor/story/0,,1713166,00.html Accessed 16 December 2007.

Rodriguez G (2007) Expelling academic's ideological crackpots. *Centre Daily Times* 2 August:A8.

Tabuenca Córdoba M S (2003) Dia-V permanente in Ciudad Juárez. *El Diario de Ciudad Juárez* 2 March:A21.

Suggested Reading

Landes J (ed) (1998) *Feminism, the Public and the Private*. Oxford: Oxford University Press. A good, multidisciplinary overview of the gendering of public and private spheres and subjects.

Tabuenca Cordóba M S and Monárrez Fragoso J (2008) *Bordeando la Violencia Contra las Mujeres en la Frontera Norte de México [Delimiting the Violence Against Women Along Mexico's Northern Border]*. Tijuana: El Colegio de la Frontera Norte. An in-depth discussion of activism and gendered violence in northern Mexico.

Chapter 5

Population, Environment, War, and Racism: Adventures of a Public Scholar

Paul R. Ehrlich

My first interest in public policy beyond US politics developed in 1950–1 when I was a sophomore at the University of Pennsylvania, rooming with two World War II veterans and reading William Vogt's *Road to Survival* and Fairfield Osborn's *Our Plundered Planet*. The discussions we had then about overpopulation and environmental deterioration had a profound impact on me. At the same time, so did reading books on evolution by Ernst Mayr (*Systematics and the Origin of Species*) and Theodosius Dobzhansky (*Genetics and the Origin of Species*) in connection with my desire to have a career studying the evolution of butterflies. The latter impacts were magnified by the increasing difficulty I was having raising butterflies from caterpillars at my New Jersey home, because overspraying with DDT for mosquito control was making plants in my neighborhood poisonous to insects.

When I went to graduate school in the Department of Entomology at the University of Kansas my first assistantship was working on the evolution of DDT resistance in fruit flies, and that deepened my concern over the toxification of the landscape and pre-adapted me to, a few years later, appreciate Rachel Carson's message in *Silent Spring*. At the time (mid-1950s) the restaurants of Lawrence, Kansas were segregated, and a faculty friend and I organized lunch time "sit-ins" of restaurants with mixed African–American and White groups. The restaurants wouldn't serve us, but they couldn't then serve others. Eventually, after death threats but no actual violence, the restaurants agreed to serve non-whites. This solidified my interest in social justice, which is a motivating force in my life even today.

When I was hired by Stanford in 1959, I was asked to teach a course in evolution. It was a 10-week course, and I spent the first 9 weeks saying where human beings had come from, and the last week saying where I thought we were going. The course was popular, and the students very much liked the last week of lectures. They told their parents about it, and soon I was asked to speak to alumni groups on the issue of the environmental future. Through one such contact, I was invited to speak to the Commonwealth Club in San Francisco in 1966. My address was on "The food from the sea myth: The biology of a red herring", and I talked about the then-current notion, long since disappeared, that the human population could keep growing forever because the resources of the sea were infinite. What I hadn't realized was that Commonwealth Club speeches are broadcast, and I soon was getting requests to speak about population issues in Bay Area radio and TV shows. Rachel Carson had stirred up the environmental movement, and as a concerned natural-born loudmouth, I could not resist taking the opportunity to speak to audiences of thousands of people rather than just dozens of students.

Around the same time, Ian Ballantine (the inventor of the paperback and founder of Ballantine Books) had been collaborating with David Brower, Executive Director of the Sierra Club, in publishing on environmental issues. They came to me and asked if what I had been saying could be put down in a short book. They thought (which shows how naïve people were then) that if such a book were published in 1968 it might influence the politics of the presidential election that year to bring more attention to environmental issues.

With the help of my wife and longtime scholarly partner, Anne Ehrlich, I wrote the book in about a month of evenings. However, Ballantine wanted the book to be single-authored, and Anne's name was removed from the final draft. They also thought our proposed title, *Population, Resources, and Environment*, was not sexy enough, and substituted *The Population Bomb* in its stead. I learned a few lessons about being a public scholar right then and there. On the negative side, I got labeled as a "population nut", even though such things as misuse of pesticides played a major role in the book. Ballantine was right on the title though: the book has sold over 3 million copies—not bad for an "academic" book. In general academics are not great choosers of titles for popular books. My own bad judgment on titles was confirmed by another event in 1969. With a close colleague, Charles Remington at Yale University, and a New Haven attorney, Richard Bowers, I founded Zero Population Growth (ZPG). The name for the organization was Bowers' idea, and I didn't like it a bit. I told him it would confuse people. But since he was the one who thought of starting an organization, we let him have his way, and he was correct. ZPG turned out to be an excellent name. Within a few years, it was ranked as the most effective lobbying group in Washington DC, and the term "zero population growth" actually infiltrated the technical demographic literature, meaning a "stationary" (that is, non-growing) population.

The next big change in my career as a public scientist came in late 1968 when Arthur Godfrey, a major celebrity of the time, sent a copy of *The Population Bomb* to Johnny Carson, host of the "Tonight Show". John was very interested in issues of population and environment, and invited me to appear on the show. To make a long story short, my first three appearances (out of 20 some) with Carson occurred in the first few months of 1969. At the time of the invitation ZPG was an organization of some six chapters and 600 people, but John allowed me to give ZPG's address in Los Altos, California, on each of the shows. By mid-1969, the organization had grown to 600 chapters and 60,000 members. The day after my first appearance on the show Los Altos had the largest mail delivery to a single address in its entire history. I learned a big lesson—you have a lot more influence talking to 15 million people at one time than the few thousand people who listen to an average Bay Area show!

One of the main dilemmas of becoming a public scholar was obvious to me from the very start of my career in the media. When I first went on television and radio, I was concerned that my colleagues would write me off as a scientist. How could I maintain a scientific reputation while dealing with the public in terms that are divorced from those used when publishing in the technical literature? If one approaches a TV interview prepared to mimic the structure of a scientific paper—introduction, materials and methods, results, and discussion—the interview would be over long before you even got to materials and methods. Sound bites of basic conclusions are what is required. But I needn't have worried. The answer is to use sound bites with the public, but to keep up your scientific work so that people cannot accuse you of being "just a popularizer".

My colleagues at Stanford had been extremely supportive of my Bay Area activities and writing of *The Population Bomb*. In fact, many of them read the manuscript, including Don Kennedy, who is now editor of *Science* and was president of Stanford University from 1980 to 1992. Peter Raven, Director of the Missouri Botanic Garden, and the former Home Secretary of the National Academy of Sciences also read it and was encouraging. It turned out that other evolutionists and ecologists were extraordinarily concerned about the deteriorating state of the world and were delighted to support me and my efforts. They were delighted that I was able to present their concerns to the "Tonight Show". And many of them themselves began to "go public" on environmental issues. Indeed, several had preceded me, notably George Woodwell at Woods Hole. The enthusiastic support of my colleagues has been a wonderful aspect of my career as a public scholar. Many of them have been extremely helpful in my media "career", especially during several years when I was a correspondent for NBC News, doing environmental stories for the "Today Show", working with the best producer in the business, Sam Hurst.

Especially in the early days, I suffered many attacks—and they continue! But like most scientists, I care not what Rush Limbaugh or Ann Coulter "think". Scientists value first and foremost their reputations with their scientific colleagues, not with the random ignoramuses that so often pop up on the airwaves. In order to protect our reputations, Anne and I have always tried to have our public statements and policy publications carefully refereed by the best scholars we know, to be sure they are as accurate as possible. This is, of course, especially important when one is doing interdisciplinary work and speaking out in areas not considered part of one's disciplinary background.

A pressing problem for public scholars is how to make it clear when one is speaking as a scientist and when one is speaking as a citizen. Several of my colleagues and I have come up with a formula for this, which I try to follow. First, inform people of the scientific consensus on an issue. Then if you differ on that issue in an area of your expertise, it is ethically correct to give your opinion but to make clear its degree of scientific heterodoxy. At the next level is giving your opinion as a citizen who has put a great deal of effort into studying an issue. For example, I have no expertise in climatology, but I have studied it intensively over the years and discussed it frequently with experts like my colleague, Stephen Schneider. Therefore, in my opinion, it is okay for me to express views on issues of climate change, as long as I make clear that I am transmitting opinions that are the result of study and discussion with experts who know the area well. Obviously, there often are not firm lines between the various levels of expertise, but one can at least make an attempt to be clear to audiences and readers how far one's views are from scholarly consensus, and what cultural baggage you may be bringing to the discussion.

Being a public scholar carries with it many burdens, but it also provides (especially for a field biologist) many benefits. Invitations to speak around the world have allowed me to carry out fieldwork in areas that would have been financially impossible for me otherwise. It's also a huge personal pleasure. It gives one the chance to observe directly environmental conditions in many places. And, most important, it gives one a chance to get feedback from people who are normally not part of a scholar's world —from attitudes of military officers on weapons of mass destruction (discovered during our research on Nuclear Winter) to attitudes on biodiversity loss from farmers. This latter feedback occurred in a joint meeting in the western Australian wheatlands. We have also received feedback from callers to "talk radio" shows enraged by the idea that there are no genetically determined intellectual differences among "races". The reactions of the public to scholarly outreach, and the failure of most decision-makers to take needed steps to ameliorate the human predicament, have been gradually shifting my research to trying to understand cultural evolution; that is, how and why humanity's non-genetic information changes over time. We must find ways to deliberately shape that evolution so that the views of those who study humanity can more readily be brought to public attention, evaluated, and where necessary, incorporated into policy.

Perhaps the biggest single academic advantage to me of being a public scholar has been the opportunity to meet and work with people in numerous other disciplines—economics, psychology, political science, history, the law, just to name a few. The good news is that disciplinary boundaries are gradually breaking down, as are prejudices about scientists speaking out on issues of public policy. And many senior environmental scientists are working hard to change our own disciplinary culture. When I was trained, the emphasis was on doing research and then letting fellow scientists know what you have found. Your science was not completed until you had "informed other researchers of your results". Now we're working to add to that ". . .and explained their importance to the general public".

Suggestions and Advice

For young environmental scientists, my main advice is twofold. One is, don't wait to get involved as a public scholar; get involved now. Time is short. Science is a social activity, and we owe it to those who support our research to disseminate the results as widely as possible. Institutions are starting to appear to encourage this—one of the first was the Aldo Leopold Leadership Program designed to train mid-level environmental scientists on how to relate to the press, public, and legislators. My second suggestion is to ignore ancient disciplinary boundaries, which trace back to the very different world of Aristotle. The environmental crisis is not going to be solved unless physical scientists, social scientists, and scholars in the humanities work hand-in-hand with biologists. The ongoing and very successful collaborations of ecologists and economists illustrate this. And the importance of the humanities in attacking problems of inequity (which must be reduced if needed cooperation is to be achieved) was long ago suggested by the role played by a novel, *Uncle Tom's Cabin*. If you happen to be employed by a university, you might even get involved in reorganizing your very conservative institution (they all are) so that it will be better able to help society achieve sustainability.

Suggested Reading

Carson R (1962) *Silent Spring*. Boston: Houghton Mifflin.
Dobzhansky T (1951) *Genetics and the Origin of Species*. 3rd edn. New York: Columbia University Press.

Ehrlich P R (1968) *The Population Bomb*. New York: Ballantine Books.

Mayr E (1942) *Systematics and the Origin of Species*. New York: Columbia University Press.

Osborn F Jr. (1948) *Our Plundered Planet*. Boston: Little, Brown and Company.

Vogt W (1948) *Road to Survival*. New York: William Sloan.

Chapter 6
The Something We Can Do

David Domke

I had no plans to be a public scholar. I became one, nonetheless, in September 2002. That month my promotion to Associate Professor with tenure at the University of Washington became official. The same month the UW's alumni magazine published a story about my research on US news coverage that followed the September 11 terrorist attacks of one year earlier. A couple of graduate students and I had found that the American press uncritically waved the flag and supported the federal government's military response, beginning in Afghanistan. In our research, we offered modest critiques of what we called an overly deferential, "patriotic press". This analysis was propelled by a belief that undergirds my interest in political communication—that independent journalism is crucial for democracy. For some alumni, however, this work smacked of anti-Americanism. Several fired off angry emails expressing a wish that the university sever its ties with me. I was taken aback, and I considered it ironic because two of my co-authors were active-duty officers in the US military attending graduate school on scholarships. Soon criticisms of my work made their way into the stone-throwing world of talk radio and Internet blogs, and I was pulled into the public arena whether I wanted to be or not. It was a shock—and a jolt of energy. Years earlier I had been a journalist, feeding off the adrenaline of news reporting. This feeling returned with the dustup over my research. I was back in the public conversation, writing, talking, defending ideas ... *engaging*. It felt good. Even better, it felt right.

What commenced was a transformation of my mindset. I now regularly write op-ed essays for newspapers as well as for internet forums, and receive plenty of emails when I do (the public, whether angry or delighted, always writes!). I deliver talks and engage in conversations in settings that range from lecture halls to union halls, from household living rooms to outdoor fairs and festivals to religious sanctuaries. I lead day-long public workshops on political communication with grassroots activists, curious citizens, and political leaders. And I have worked for causes and on electoral campaigns, sometimes side by side with students of mine. To be clear, I do these things in addition to my responsibilities as a faculty member. I thrive on the dynamic discovery process involved in teaching, and I publish research in peer-reviewed journals because I find it intellectually energizing and I believe in the scholarly enterprise. It's as if I have two jobs, one as a professor and one as a citizen. I used to believe that the former amply encompassed the latter, but today I think differently. The teaching and research that occur in university settings matter tremendously, but these institutions are the educational equivalent of gated communities. Not all people can or want to gain entrance. I am now committed to working with people on both sides of the gates.

Growing Pains

My outlook crystallized with a book that documented and critiqued the religious rhetoric of the Bush administration and the response of US news media between September 11, 2001, and the Iraq War in spring 2003.[1] I published portions of this research in academic journals, yet thought a book might reach a wider audience. It did: the book came out smack in the middle of the 2004 presidential election, and it gained public attention in a manner well beyond any of my publications in academic outlets. I was invited to speak in a number of public contexts. I wrote op-eds for leading newspapers and for sites around the internet. I was interviewed by leading national and international reporters. I learned to speak in sound bites and experienced the terror of being interviewed live by unsympathetic broadcast anchors. Students studying abroad said they saw me on television in Hungary. A colleague heard me on the BBC. My sister caught me on CNN. It felt like I went from 0 to 60 overnight. My life has not stayed at this Chomskyian pace, but neither has it returned to idle: it's more like I am going 40 or so with moments of overdrive. It turns out that news media and the public have an insatiable interest in religion and politics—and for good reason, because their intertwining profoundly matters, especially in a nation as powerful as the United States. I fully realize that I just happen to be caught in something big. Still, I am part of the conversation.

I did not realize, though, how challenging all of this can be. In particular, two aspects of public scholarship caught me off guard. The first is the nature of the conversation. In the research culture of academia, disagreements and emotions tend to be couched in genteel terms and nuanced positions are prized. Not everyone adheres to these rules of engagement, but among scholars it is uncommon to tell someone straight out "You're wrong", it is even more rare to exhibit strong emotion, and the best answer almost always is "You know, I don't think there's any one right answer". The underlying dimension that connects these pieces is a posture of detachment, an I-just-study-this, I'm-not-overly-invested-in-how-this-turns-out positionality. I have found that the general public despises such aloofness—because they rightly recognize it as a position of privilege. In contrast, for those who turn out to hear or talk with scholars, the topics at hand often are everyday realities. Here's one example: I am interested in how US politicians and news media have responded to the rising power of Christian conservatives in recent decades. For me, this is what I study. But for citizens it is far more. As a result, it is true yet inadequate for me to tell a concerned parent that the push by some politicians to have biblical creationism taught alongside evolution in public schools is a political maneuver; for this parent, the issue cuts to the core of their values and what their child's future looks like. Detached, nuanced analysis doesn't cut it for them in such moments.

A second lesson I have learned is that talking with the public requires a process of translation: one in which complex ideas are converted into words, images, and examples unburdened by scholarly jargon. Such a public voice is perceived by some academics to be a "dumbing down", a stripping away of sophisticated intellectual material in order to reach a lowbrow public. I see this process differently. Average citizens don't speak the language of the academy for simple reasons: they haven't spent years learning it, or perhaps they did but now they don't like such communication. If I genuinely want to talk with them, I need to work at developing a common vocabulary. Sometimes this occurs only through painful trial and error. When my book was published, I was convinced that my pre-graduate school work as a journalist and my position as a professor of Communication gave me an edge in writing in a style comfortable for the public. Surely I could do this, I thought. Then a friend and public ally gently asked one day over lunch if I was open to some feedback. I promptly was informed that portions of the book were tough sledding—I believe the word she used was "inaccessible". When I heard something similar from another friend, I broke into a cold sweat. By the time a third person shared this view, it was time to either find new friends or realize that while my intentions were good, I still had miles to go to become a *public* scholar.

In both cases I underestimated my immersion in the culture of academia. When citizens become confused or frustrated with our detachment and nuanced positions, big words and five-semicolon sentences, our tendency is to dismiss the public as inferior. This is a mistake of the first order. When a doctor explains a disease in terms incomprehensible to a patient or exhibits an impersonal bedside manner, we recognize that the blame resides with the doctor. When a lawyer offers an inscrutable legal assessment to a client or expresses little concern for the person behind the case, we know the lawyer is at fault. These professionals offer something that the public wants, indeed even needs, and they have a responsibility to deliver it in a useful manner. It's no different with scholars. We have frameworks, ideas, insights—all of which engender unique vantage points, ones marked by reflections that the average citizen does not have the time or inclination to undertake. In turn, we have a duty, a social responsibility, to offer these perspectives in lay terms for those who are interested. Please allow me to put this in distinctly personal terms. I am a tenured professor at a major university, with a modest-but-comfortable salary funded by taxpaying citizens. I live in a highly affluent nation that is the world's leading superpower. In short, I am a walking embodiment of privilege. It is not acceptable for me to write for and teach only the few who attend my university or read the academic journals I publish in. I owe the public more.

People and Hope

My faculty appointment is in the Department of Communication, which was formed from two academic units in 2002. In creating the Department, faculty in the former units considered our joint strengths, looked at trends in education, and contemplated what might be our unifying principles. An idea emphasized by the Re-Envisioning the PhD Project, funded by Pew Charitable Trusts, caught our attention: the importance of preparing graduate students for a range of careers, including many outside the academy. With only a modest sense of where this might lead us, we created a series of mini-seminars on professional pathways and installed a core graduate class titled "Community scholarship and public life". Known as The Public Scholarship Course, this is a defining piece of our program: it attracts students, has forced faculty to decide how public scholarship matters for promotion and other institutional rewards, and serves as the ever-present nudge that all institutions need. I took my first crack at teaching the course in 2007—and wrote this essay while I did so, with students offering thoughts in response.[2] My students and I conducted workshops with local teenagers, worked on translating academic ideas into a public voice, and pursued teaching and research opportunities with grade-school children, university alumni, and a nonprofit environmental organization. At all times the emphasis was on talking with and listening to people who are not university faculty or students—that is, those who don't experience the world as an abstract curiosity that compels systematic analysis. Such interactions reminded us, deeply reminded us, of a crucial truth: there are people behind the data.

This is a point I have learned over and over in workshops on political strategy and communication that I conduct with a University of Washington colleague. The two of us work together because we enjoy and learn from one another, and also because we find the solidarity empowering. Early in our partnership we hit upon an effective way to end our workshops—by invoking three moments that changed the course of history: the writing of the Declaration of Independence, the refusal by

Rosa Parks to give up her seat on a bus, and the wearing of a red ribbon to bring a visibility to the AIDS crisis. In these instances, my colleague and I say, people accomplished something momentous by embracing the moment at hand. These individuals did what they could, when they had the chance. Following a workshop one Saturday, a participant noted that Rosa Parks could not have had the same impact sitting on her front porch; instead, she had to get on a bus and, with the support of like-minded others, demand to be treated with dignity. It was a learning moment I carry with me and share with others. I am compelled to leave the safety of my academic porch, to enter the public arena and to take a position. On the wall of my office I have framed these words of Helen Keller: "I am only one; but still I am one. I cannot do everything, but I can do something; I will not refuse to do the something I can do". Perhaps that is what defines a public scholar: a determination to do the something that we can do.

In the end, my goal is to help people and organizations understand how political and media systems work. With such insight, all of us can better make sense of why certain political and news messages emerge, why some of these persuade the public and shape policy, and why some gain no traction whatsoever. In the ideal world, individuals equipped with this knowledge might learn to navigate systems effectively—or, in the best of all outcomes, to find ways to make them more democratic. More knowledge is always better. Even still, the best public scholarship is about more than the imparting of knowledge; it's also about providing hope, even inspiration. Hope is a word that is almost entirely absent from the academic lexicon. Why? Because to talk of hope suggests that we might care, that we might be genuinely invested in the material that we research and teach about. Public scholarship and hope go hand in hand. When scholars highlight opportunities for social change, we offer hope. When scholars help people to negotiate systems in ways that more fully honor their humanity, we offer hope. When scholars provide tools that allow people to take greater control over personal and cultural choices, we offer hope. And when scholars drop our detachment and adopt an ethic of engagement, we offer hope. It is this emphasis—on the belief that together we can build a better world, a more perfect union of humanity—that drives me toward public scholarship.

The rewards can be great for all involved. I'll conclude by providing one example. I was invited in 2005 to speak at the western region meeting for the Democratic Party National Committee (DNC). The DNC was looking for insights about how to promote the party's ideals. Democrats had lost control of the US Congress to the Republican Party in 2002, and the Democratic candidate was defeated in the US presidential election in 2004 for the seventh time in 10 elections. There were signs, however, that the western United States was trending increasingly Democratic, a potential shift that was part of a "50-state strategy" launched by new party chair Howard Dean.[3] Now Democratic leaders in 13 western US states—the area of the nation in which I lived—needed ideas. I realized that I had some. This represented a new threshold for me: activity with a distinctly partisan bent. I worked on how best to communicate my thoughts and ideas. I decided not only to share some research findings and reflections, the typical scholarly approach, but also to bring a list of suggestions for the party leaders—a short, bullet-pointed list. I opened with a story about my family's past support for the Democratic Party, to show that I cared. And I put my presentation into a simple-to-digest visual format and showed a video clip to illustrate my claims. A year earlier, I would have done none of these. I may not even have accepted the invitation to speak.

That presentation initiated a dynamic set of relationships. I now am asked to do workshops with Democratic Party officials and candidates on effective communication techniques. For these, I share both the findings of my research and the translations I undertake in my public engagement. In exchange, I have gained a window into the strategic processes that drive American politics—a core component of what I study in my scholarly work. These insights have produced new research findings, which in turn provide material for my academic and public scholarship. In addition, through these contacts some of my students have had the chance to research and work in political campaign contexts. And one final unexpected thing has occurred: along the way I lost and then developed anew my sense of professional identity. Was I a professor who was sticking his foot in the public waters of politics? Was I becoming a political hack who happened to have a good day job at a university? Public scholarship, like any unforeseen or untraditional career move, provided an opportunity for personal and professional reflection. That's never bad. This is who I have decided I am: an educator whose classroom is much bigger than I expected and where the learning flows in multiple directions from many sources. It's the road less traveled, and I'm fortunate to have found it.

Endnotes

[1] The book is *God Willing? Political Fundamentalism in the White House, the "War on Terror," and the Echoing Press* (2004, London: Pluto Press).

[2] For their contributions to my thinking about public scholarship, I wish to thank Peg Achterman, Fahed Al-Sumait, Vanessa Au, Laura Busch, Toby Campbell, Carol Coe, Damon Dicicco, Deen Freelon, Valerie Gilbert, Kristin Gustafson, Tabitha Hart, Li Liu, Jamie Moshin, Michele Poff, and Penelope Sheets. In addition, special thanks to Lynne Baab and Michael Coe.

[3] Dean was elected chairman of the DNC on 12 February 2005. The 50-state strategy is featured on the DNC's website (accessed on 15 November 2006) at http://www.democrats.org/a/party/a_50_state_strategy. In Dean's words, "Election by election, state by state, precinct by precinct, door by door, vote by vote ... we're going to lift our party up and take this country back for the people who built it". It's an electoral

approach that clashed with some party leaders who wanted to target party resources to distinctly identified candidates and contests, rather than across all electoral contexts.

Suggested Reading

Novick P (1988) *That Noble Dream: The "Objectivity Question" and the American Historical Profession.* Cambridge: Cambridge University Press.

McChesney RW (2007) *Communication Revolution: Critical Junctures and the Future of Media.* New York: New Press.

Lakoff G (2002) *Moral Politics: How Liberals and Conservatives Think.* 2nd edn. Chicago: University of Chicago Press.

These three books influenced my thinking on public scholarship. In each of these, the authors do two things: (1) discuss an important scholarly matter in substantive terms, with careful, thoughtful analysis, and (2) offer insights for how scholars might bring their knowledge into the public arena in useful ways. It's a powerful combination, written in a compelling manner.

Chapter 7

Philadelphia Dreaming: Discovering Citizenship between the University and the Schools

Julia Reinhard Lupton

My twin sister Ellen and I were born in Philadelphia in 1963. "Philadelphia" means love of those who come from the same womb (*delph-*). Translated as "brotherly love", *Philadelphia*, like its Latinate cousin "fraternity", renders political friendship in familial terms. My early career as a psychoanalytic critic focused in part on the psychic pleasures and costs of *philadelphia* (as incest and fratricide). At mid career, largely due to my work with public schools, my interests turned to *philadelphia* as citizenship, but without relinquishing the affective and erotic lining of the word. Along the way, I gave birth to four children, including triplets, who daily test the frontiers of *philadelphia* in everything they do. In a variety of scenes both strictly academic and more experimental and domestic, I am in search of ways to zone and rezone *philadelphia* for my students, my readers, my family, and myself.

By far the most transformative public work in my academic life was the founding of Humanities Out There (HOT), an educational partnership between the School of Humanities at the University of California, Irvine and a local, largely Latino school district in nearby Santa Ana. In the spring of 1997, I was enjoying the first fruits of tenure and the challenges of new motherhood. When I received a lunch invitation from my Dean and my Associate Dean, I had no idea that my professional life was about to change forever. Over soup and salad, the deans asked me to organize outreach efforts for the School of Humanities. A few weeks later, I found myself launching HOT. With the support of our next dean and several visionaries on campus and off, the program has survived sea changes in state funding and outreach nomenclature in order to become a model for university-community engagement at UCI and across the nation. During 10 years of this work with schools, I found myself alternately challenged, exhilarated and exhausted, but the final impact has been a genuine change in every aspect of my professional life, from my writing and teaching styles (clearer, more direct, more grounded), to my vision of the university's relationship to the community (it should be reciprocal, serious, and sustained). Although I have begun exiting this work in order to take on new opportunities, my work with the HOT program remains an essential chapter and a fundamental turning point in my intellectual autobiography.

The basic model of HOT is simple: a graduate student and a team of undergraduates go into a Santa Ana classroom 15 times over the course of the year, executing a content-rich sequence of humanities exercises designed in collaboration with host teachers. The graduate student writes the lesson and provides a brief overview. Undergraduates then work with small groups of students to develop the material through active reading, writing, and discussion. Using funds from a grant from the National Endowment for the Humanities, we select the most promising exercises for further editing and publication in print and on CDs.

This model took years to develop. In our early years, it was hip to be HOT. The program bore a distinctly ad hoc and experimental profile: some activities occurred in after-school programs, some were tied to performances, and some led to the publication of an anthology or play script. Workshops were scattered across the grades, spanning elementary, intermediate and high school classrooms in several districts. The mix was exciting, but it was also a mess: hard to evaluate, hard to supervise, and sometimes hard to sell. Over the years, largely thanks to our collaboration with another program on campus, the UCI History-Social Science Project, we learned to focus our energies on school-day activities in intermediate and high-school classrooms in Santa Ana. All workshops are now based on the California State Content Standards, and we work hard to match our activities with what teachers are already doing in their classrooms.

The ultimate exemplar of *philadelphia* in the classical tradition is Antigone. Her loyalty to her brother Polyneices is so great that in the very opening scene of the play, she rejects her quieter sister Ismene. Antigone and Ismene represent two faces of citizenship: on the one hand, the power of civil disobedience to restructure the fabric of a polity, often at the expense of the freedom or even life of its proponents; on the other hand, a normative and pragmatic investment in the rule of the law and the transmission of values. In the words of a brilliant recent study of the play, "It is Ismene who responds appropriately to things as they are, while Antigone, dismissing all but kinship, acts outside her means" (Tyrrell and Bennett 1998:38). The play attempts to integrate these two models of citizenship; as she moves towards death, Antigone also moves towards the polis whose interests she has come to represent.

Sophocles' sisters have been a part of HOT since our inception. One of our very first projects was to bring a student performance of *Antigone* to the UCI campus. The director was a former student of mine, Stephanie Keefer, who had double-majored in English and theatre at

UC Irvine. I ran into her at Santa Ana High School when I had just begun the HOT program, and she told me about her new staging of *Antigone*. The performance was bilingual, with passages declaimed in both Spanish and English. Antigone was cast as an Aztec princess, and Creon appeared as a *conquistador*. Stephanie brought the cast to UCI to perform selected scenes for an audience of undergraduates. It was a galvanizing moment for the program, as we witnessed an act of *philadelphia* occurring between languages, cultures, and institutions.

When we shifted our focus from performances and temporary installations to developing curricula for English and history classrooms, *Antigone* continued to inspire us. One of my graduate students wrote an excellent unit on "Global Antigones", stressing the civil disobedience line in the play and showing how it has been staged in distinctive political contexts, from democratic Athens to Vichy France to *apartheid* South Africa. The unit reframes a classical text in a series of dynamic frames in order to unlock its political and philosophical potentialities for young readers today. The approach both encourages identification with the teen-aged Antigone's rebellious attitude towards Creon, and challenges students to embed these affective responses in reflections on their own civic and domestic situations.[1]

Through our classroom interventions, our work with graduate and undergraduate students, and our publication of humanities curricula for K-12 classrooms, HOT has generated a set of "citizenship papers", in several senses: a set of papers or readings that address citizenship as theme and problem; a distinctive protocol or way of reading these papers; and, finally, the larger goal of creating circles of citizenship, formal and informal, among diverse groups of interlocutors.

First, "citizenship papers" implies "a canon", a set of "papers" or readings on and around the topic of education for citizenship. Graduate students involved in the program (eight each year) enroll in a graduate seminar, "Humanities and the public sphere". We read major statements on the history and theory of education, especially as problems of pedagogy bear on concepts of citizenship and civil society. Standard players include John Dewey, Jane Addams, Paulo Freire, and Howard Gardner. The readings are extremely short—sometimes we're reading a concept as much as an author—and we approach the assignments not as we would in a literature or history seminar (for their contexts, rhetoric, arguments, or place in disciplinary scholarship) but more immediately, for the practical wisdom they might offer about what we are doing each week in Santa Ama classrooms.

Then there are the materials we teach in our HOT workshops, much of which we go on to publish and distribute as curricular guides. The texts and topics here are generated largely by the California State Content Standards, a massive list of skill sets and subject areas mandating what must be taught at each grade level in each discipline. After several

years of negotiating with teachers, their principals, and the school
district, these Content Standards emerged as an intellectually responsible
template of topics that could help both sides of the partnership—
the schools and the university—arrive at legitimate and legible areas
for shared inquiry and collaborative teaching. (My first advice to any
university person wanting to initiate a school-based project would be:
find the web page for your state Department of Education and find out
what their content standards are! The time you spend will pay off in
credibility, mutual respect, institutional welcome, and better decision-
making.)

The phrase "citizenship papers" also implies "a set of protocols",
not just texts to be read, but ways to read them. In the graduate
seminar, this has meant approaching texts by Locke, Addams or Dewey
in a manner that is immediate, practical and problem based, yet still
intellectually serious. So too, undergraduate tutors preparing to teach a
session on hospitality in the *Odyssey* or Islam in medieval Africa are
not just absorbing the material as they would in an academic course;
they are exercising their wits in order to figure out how to share these
materials with their cohort of students in the schools. (And most of the
undergraduates love it, coming back quarter after quarter in order to feel
the special rush, part cognitive and part theatrical, that only teaching
delivers.) The humanities are not just about *studying* multiple forms of
literacy and cognition, but also about *exercising* those forms in diverse
contexts towards distinctive ends. The humanities involve *doing* and
making as well as *thinking*.

Finally, "citizenship papers" implies "a vision or goal". Citizenship
procedures, whether they are the laws of naturalization or the rituals
and routines of public education, aim to *produce citizens*, persons
who achieve a measure of formal equality within a shared space
of mobility, interchange, and collective decision-making. Establishing
shared narratives along with ways of reading them is one piece in the
work of building citizens, what Amy Koritz (2005:82) calls "enriching
the commons of our society". In inter-institutional programs like HOT,
this citizen-building project is multilateral, drawing all participants from
both institutions into its civic processes. On the university side, any
humanities classroom is a potentially civic space, insofar as a group
comes together to study the varieties of human interaction according
to a recognized set of rules and procedures for dialogue and debate.
Amy Koritz makes the case for literature: "Precisely because literature
is intuitively accessible to students without huge amounts of technical or
contextual expertise and is inextricable in its content from the question
of how individuals live together, it is better positioned than many other
disciplines, and particularly the sciences, to reconnect with the world in
precisely these ways" (9). This civic dimension is necessarily intensified
when the program of study involves moving between distinct settings,

working collaboratively, and experiencing diversity of every sort (racial, linguistic, economic), at every juncture (in the schools, but also in the university setting, where our undergraduate and graduate student participants are more ethnically diverse than the university at large). The civic point here is not the cultivation of difference, which is everywhere about us, but rather building commonality, "circles of citizenship" where people really can and do talk and work together on shared projects.

As for the schools, like any sites of public education, the classrooms we visit have as part of their explicit mandate the civic education of their students. The situation we enter in Santa Ana differs from other environments, however, in that many of the students we work with are either not citizens themselves, or are the children of non-citizens. Building the linguistic, logical, critical, and expressive skills of these young people as well as increasing their access to a fund of narratives both literary and historical concerning immigration, nation-building, and social action may help them achieve political and economic naturalization for themselves or their families. Moreover, studying in small discussion groups with college students from diverse backgrounds, who represent a different point in the educational system and another location in the socio-economic landscape, is in and of itself civic, for both parties, regardless of the content taught or the ends sought. Building intellectual communities is a recurrent theme in our units, whether it is a lesson on medieval monasteries, a unit on early American church design, or a lesson on abolition that uses the mastheads of abolitionist newspapers to introduce students to the power of print. From our several constituencies we aim to develop scholar-citizens, equipped to address issues of contemporary urgency through historical analysis, cultural self-consciousness, and the arts of eloquence—the pillars of humanistic inquiry.

It should come as no surprise that I think departments of literature and history should be doing more of this kind of work. I am not alone. For example, *Greater Expectations* (http://www.greaterexpectations.org/), the report on undergraduate liberal arts and general education published by the American Association of Colleges and Universities in 2001, speaks repeatedly about the need for more problem-based learning, fieldwork, and education for the business of life in the twenty-first century. At the graduate level, the Responsive PhD Initiative launched by the Woodrow Wilson National Fellowship Foundation (http://www.woodrow.org/) calls for "public scholarship that applies academic expertise to social challenges", along with "vigorous efforts to open the doctorate to new populations ... and clearer professional paths for PhDs both within and beyond research universities". Imagining America: Artists and Scholars in Public Life (http://www.ia.umich.edu/) is a national consortium of universities dedicated to expanding public scholarship at all levels of the academy, from community colleges to Research I universities, from undergraduates to graduate students and faculty. (Notice that foundations and national think-tanks seem more able to think outside the box than traditional departments.)

Finally, a coda: although I've been making a case for the civic dimensions of working with schools, it is also important to note here that this kind of activity is less directly and immediately civic than other more project-based interventions, whether conducted within the arts and humanities (such as the Arts of Citizenship, http://www. artsofcitizenship.umich.edu/, a program at the University of Michigan) or via social-science-based programs that work with politics and activism as such (as in the Center for Democracy and Citizenship, http://www.publicwork.org, at the University of Minnesota[2]). Although HOT may have begun in the defiant shadow of Antigone, it has crossed over into the more normative institutional sphere of her sister Ismene. Why, then, the emphasis on schools, if other forms of public scholarship are actually more civic?

Working with schools on curricula is a natural development for the humanities: it gives us an immediate content base, as well as a career path for many of our undergraduates, which makes the movement between institutions both invigorating and familiar, stretching our horizons outwards in order to pull them back in for tighter and more focused study. As Amy Koritz argues (2005:83, citing Robert Scholes), "the humanities are fundamentally and at their core concerned with teaching". Yet, in our drive for professional recognition, Research I institutions have largely turned the task of teaching the next generation of teachers over to education departments, who in turn often lack the resources and interests in teaching the academic disciplines that their candidates need to master. A program like HOT strives to acknowledge, reintegrate, and conceptualize the deep structural and philosophical connections between teaching, research and service in the humanities, not in order to dilute or downgrade our research activities in favor of teaching or service, but rather to increase the quality, urgency, integrity, and credibility of the humanities both on campus and off. Antigone's crash-and-burn commitment to the deep particularism of cultic kinship may end up being a less enabling political model than Ismene's gentle pragmatism within the choral framework of the polity.

Working with schools, during the school day, on mandated curricula, necessarily pulls civic engagement projects towards the center. Although I see this work as deeply progressive, I am not, I confess, embarked on a radical pedagogy. I am constitutionally an Ismene, not an Antigone. And the recourse to Sophocles is telling here as well: unlike many of my colleagues elsewhere in the country involved in civic engagement, I am at least as interested in producing innovative materials on canonical texts as I am in widening the multicultural field—although the approach we develop to canonical works strives to place them in challenging and original frameworks so that their urgency can be re-examined and restored. Nonetheless, the normative character of this work—and citizenship as a discourse has a deeply normative strain—is not to everyone's liking. But I prefer to create a sustainable structure, legible and credible on several institutional fronts, that can make some real difference in the lives of actual schools and students, then to invest in temporary experiments that often fail to translate the radical politics of the academy into terms that make sense, and make change, "out there".

None of this is free, and most of us don't want to hear about it anyway. My thoughts on the resource question are simple: if we tie professional development activities for graduate students firmly to innovative programs for undergraduates, the costs start to balance out a bit. UCI's program, for example, buys eight graduate students a year out of their regular teaching, no cheap package; but we also provide the only academically integrated service learning program for undergraduates in the humanities, and this sweetens the deal considerably. Moreover, if we use content standards and other external templates in order to meet genuine needs among our partners, we can raise some of the money externally. (HOT receives about half of its budget from UCI, and half from outside sources.) In short, funding problems can be solved if there is a real will and interest to solve them.

Breaking through the inertia and defensiveness of our colleagues is another matter. Demonstrating that work we do off campus clarifies and strengthens rather than dilutes our research is one key to changing institutional attitudes. That means engaging our smartest, most ambitious, most dexterous students and faculty in this work, and rewarding them for it. We also need to build intellectually and institutionally responsible structures, relying on content standards and related measures to give structure, substance, and sustainability to our practices. Finally, we need to think hard about the civic dimensions of the work that we already do in order to bring those features forward and develop them into independent strands of activity, reinforcing and refining rather than dumbing down our research interests. Confronting the educational and civic dimensions of the humanities will ultimately, I believe, strengthen, not weaken, the disciplines. Working with schools need not devolve into mere window dressing, though the humanities could use some good PR these days. Done properly, working with schools can and should be directly linked to the themes and goals that animate the study of literature and history, constituting part of the portfolio of "citizenship papers" that make great universities into good neighbors (to the communities we live in) and good sisters (to the institutions whose goals we share).

Endnotes

[1] My thanks to Jane Newman (Professor of Comparative Literature) and to Mrilini Chakravorty (graduate student in English) for helping develop these materials in the context of HOT.

[2] On the Center for Democracy and Citizenship, see Boyte (2004).

References

Boyte H C (2004) *Everyday Politics: Reconnecting Citizens and Public Life.* Philadelphia: University of Pennsylvania Press.

Koritz A (2005) Beyond teaching tolerance: Literary studies in a democracy. *Professions*: 80–91.

Tyrrell W B and Bennett L J (1998) *Recapturing Sophocles' Antigone.* Oxford: Rowman and Littlefield.

Chapter 8

Beyond Positivism: Public Scholarship in Support of Health

Dennis Raphael

"You can take the boy out of Brooklyn, but you can't take the Brooklyn out of the boy."

"I think what you are doing is great. But I have to tell you that there are some members of the department that are concerned about your activity."

Introduction

In 1963, at the tender age of 12, my grade 6 teacher in PS 226 in Brooklyn, New York explained that under socialism the primary institutions of a society would be under public control, thereby serving the interests of the majority of the population. At that time, this made intuitive sense to me. It wasn't until 30 years later, upon obtaining a limited-term appointment to an academic health sciences department, that I realized that this insight could be applied within the academic sphere in the service of the public's health. And it was another 10 years—upon the receipt of tenure and promotion to full professor at York University—before I felt assured that taking a critical perspective to public health issues would not be a career-threatening move. Did adopting a critical perspective hinder achievement of a secure academic position? I think not. Indeed, it was adoption of this perspective and my entrance into a profoundly underdeveloped area of inquiry that—combined with the political times—enabled me to secure my current academic position.

Beginnings

There were few Jewish adults in the Brooklyn New York of the 1950s who did not have a direct or indirect association with the progressive movements of the 1930s and 1940s. At the same time, there were few who did not have an underlying fear that these associations could be used against them in the witch-hunting political atmosphere of the 1950s. Nevertheless, the left-leaning tendencies of the dominant Democratic and Liberal Parties in New York City provided space for belief in, and application of, somewhat progressive and forward-looking social policies. Thus the seeds of a public scholar were sown.

And not surprisingly—considering the ideas we were exposed to at home and at school—and with the ambivalent support of my parents, both my brother Robert and I were caught up with the civil rights and Vietnam political movements of the 1960s. I helped close my high school during the 1968 Vietnam Moratorium and visited my nation's capital for the first and last time to attend the major demonstration there. I also had my first experience of Canada by attending the *Hemispheric Conference to End the Vietnam War* in Montreal in 1968. These anti-war activities continued through my undergraduate years at Brooklyn College from 1968 to 1972.

It is a testament to the power of the dominant academic discourse that these political interests existed in a parallel yet separate universe from my study of psychology at Brooklyn College. I can recall learning and internalizing the view that psychology as a discipline was "scientific", while the sociology my brother Robert studied was somewhat suspect in that regard. While he and I both pored over *The Power Elite* by Mills (1956), *Who Rules America* by Dumhoff (1967), and even the Canadian *Vertical Mosaic* by Porter (1965), the notion that these kinds of works could contribute to an academic career devoted to understanding and improving society did not exist for me. Such was the case for the next 20 years.

Academics and the Parallel Universe of Political Activity

From the time I received my doctorate in educational psychology (1975) until my term appointment to the Department of Behavioural Science at the University of Toronto (1993), I followed a rather narrow academic track in both my research and my teaching. My research interests—carried out as a manager (research officer) of studies rather than as a titled academic (professor)—focused on adolescent personality development, teacher training, and measurement and evaluation. For example, I was interested in the assessment of teacher and individual factors shaping student achievement in mathematics and science. I also taught a wide range of psychology courses as an extramural instructor in various institutions during those years. These courses included child and adolescent development, educational psychology, and personality and psychopathology.

At the same time, however, I never failed to become involved with the federal, provincial, and municipal election campaigns of Canada's social democratic party, the New Democratic Party (NDP). Indeed, I met my wife Toba Bryant while working on the 1987 provincial election campaign. I certainly saw a connection between human development and school achievement and the social environments to which people were exposed. It was just that the connection between my scholarly work and my political interests could not be made explicit. The psychology in which I was trained made little room for academic consideration of the structural issues that shape the distribution of resources within societies, structural issues that, I began to learn, shaped the health of the public.

The Canada of the 1970s in general, and the Ontario of the 1970s in particular, did not draw attention to economic and social inequities. Federal Canadian political governance flipped from one rather benevolent political party (the Liberal) back to the other (Progressive Conservative). The province of Ontario had been ruled by the same political party (Progressive Conservative) since the 1940s. These conservatives were not of the current US variety, but rather progressive and thoughtful representatives of a tradition more common to Europe. Indeed, their political persuasions led to their being termed "Red Tories". I recall thinking upon my immigrating to Canada in the 1970s that if these were Conservatives, then what would governance by the New Democrats look like? And indeed, there was an answer to this question.

The social democratic predecessors of the New Democrats—the Cooperative Commonwealth Confederation (CCF)—had won a series of elections in the province of Saskatchewan during the 1940s and 1950s and had brought in a wide range of reforms that were adopted across Canada. Under the leadership of Premier Tommy Douglas, these reforms included socialized medicine, public pensions, human rights codes, and a range of labour-supporting policies that served to smooth the rough edges of Canadian capitalism. British Columbia frequently elected New Democrats to govern, and Manitoba and Saskatchewan continued to alternate social democratic governments with the more traditional capitalist parties. They still continue to do so with rather less to show for it as compared to the Tommy Douglas CCF.

Enter the 1990s: Exposure to the Critical Sociology of Health and the Common Sense Revolution

I gained entry—via a five-year term appointment—into the Department of Behavioural Science of the University of Toronto by way of involvement with the University's Centre for Health Promotion. The director of the centre was Irving Rootman, a sociologist. In the way of thinking favoured by the Centre, health promotion was seen as the process by which people are enabled to gain control over their health. Furthermore, one important means that scholars and others had of assisting this process was by advocating for public policy in support of health.

In addition to Rootman, the Department of Behavioural Science at the University of Toronto contained a number of critical sociologists whose focus was on health. This psychologist was not in Kansas anymore! Three of these sociologists, Ann Robertson, Joan Eakin, and David Coburn, had an especially great influence on me.

Upon my arrival, Ann Robertson and I co-taught a PhD seminar in research methodology. While I was recommending Kerlinger's *Foundations of Behavioural Research* (1986), Ann recommended John Wilson's *Social Theory* (1983), Sylvia Tesh's *Hidden Arguments: Political Ideology and Disease Prevention Policy* (1990), and Sandra Harding's *Feminism and Methodology: Social Science Issues* (1987). Suddenly, Positivism, with its capital "P" assumptions of objectivity and neutrality, and its stubborn focus on the concrete and observable, was not the only game in town.

Critical sociology brought alternative paradigms into play, and my intellectual landscape became more exciting by the moment. Joan Eakin, for example, led a program of qualitative research that directly confronted the dominant positivist research paradigm. She built upon the epistemological starting point of *idealism*, which focuses on the meanings and interpretations individuals give to their experiences and how these are embedded in their everyday lives. Gaining such understandings is vital since things perceived as real can be real in their consequences.

David Coburn was the resident advocate of *realism* in his studies of the political economy of health. Theories founded on *realism* eschew the focus upon the concrete and observable and strive to identify the underlying structures that determine the distribution of economic, social, and political resources within a society, as well as the understandings that people have about these distributions. And tied up in these conceptions were research methodologies of action science, action research, and participatory research. After engaging with these colleagues I felt I could now apply Marx's dictum: *The philosophers have attempted to explain the world in various ways. The point is to change it.*

Suddenly, my personal, scholarly study of health could also be the political study of health! And such an insight came none too soon, as the mid 1990s saw the importation of neoliberal and neoconservative ideology into Canada on a scale never before seen. All levels of government began to drastically curtail the resources made available to citizens in general and the vulnerable in particular. In Canada, the not-so-liberal Liberals in Ottawa and the not-so-progressive Conservative Party in Ontario slashed program spending at the same time they reduced corporate and income taxes for the well-off. In Ontario, this all-out assault on the welfare state was termed "The Common Sense Revolution".

Things truly appeared to be falling apart. In 1996, in the midst of it all, Richard Wilkinson's book, *Unhealthy Societies: The Afflictions of Inequality* was published. This book documented in great detail the social disintegration that had occurred in the UK as a result of nearly 20 years of Thatcherite rule. The parallel between what happened in the UK and what was happening in Canada was striking. Is this what we really wanted for Canada? I refocused my work with a new urgency.

Becoming a Public Scholar

I shifted my research towards examination of the influences upon the quality of life of individuals and communities as understood by community members, service providers, and policymakers themselves. One particularly important aspect of this work was interviewing the city councillor, regional councillor, and member of the provincial legislature from my own neighbourhood who all happened to be members of the New Democratic Party. Their structural analysis of neighbourhood issues was in stark contrast to those held by Liberal representatives interviewed from the other neighbourhood in the study (Raphael et al 2001).

I considered my findings within a critical social science perspective that took in issues of public policy, power, and class relations, and the impact of the decline of the welfare state. The results of my research appeared in refereed journals and in numerous popular publications. I began to receive invitations from a number of civil society organizations to share my findings.

Yet, despite my carefully crafted lectures and public presentations, and published papers deftly outlining the similarities between the unfolding scenes in Canada with what was happening in the UK, the healthcare and public health communities showed little interest in my work. Indeed, instead of raising the alarm about the profoundly negative health and quality of life effects of emerging neoliberal policies, governments—with the enthusiastic support of the healthcare and public health communities—threw hundreds of millions of dollars into attacks on "unhealthy lifestyle choices". Rather than look at all of the obvious structural implications of emerging policy approaches—evidenced in the deterioration in a variety of social determinants of health such as income, housing and food security, and social exclusion—they emphasized the deficiencies of the individual who was seen as making unhealthy "choices"!

What did positivist psychology have to say about all of these developments? *Nothing.* Even sub-disciplines of psychology such as health psychology and community psychology were strangely reluctant to examine social structures, issues of power and dominance, and how public policy shaped the distribution of economic and social resources that shaped health. My life as a psychologist gradually ended.

Luckily, my new armoury of knowledge in critical social theory, the political economy of health, and the sociology of knowledge provided me with the tools to understand how this situation had come about and what could be done in response. So, like any other concerned citizen with a modicum of knowledge and analytical skills, I began to publicize what I saw happening. In the past, the UN had lauded Canada as one of the best places to live in the world. But with the neoliberal onslaught and the rapid disintegration of its social structures in support of health, the UN was now attacking Canada's lack of response to the poverty and inequality in its midst. Indeed, a reoccurring event became one of UN committees lambasting Canada for refusing to meet its commitments under various international human rights and social development covenants. I began to write op-ed pieces in the papers. I published refereed articles on the impact of income and wealth inequality on Canadians' health and well-being. I was invited to address civil society organizations. I taught students about the emerging literature on the political economy of health. For these efforts, I received shaded warnings about these activities from university authorities.

Safe Landing and Going On the Road

In 2001, almost miraculously, the "other" university in Toronto, York University, started up a School of Health Policy and Management. With over 100 publications, numerous research grants, and an excellent teaching record, York saw no reason not to hire me. Indeed, my activities in trying to influence public policy and public understandings of health determinants was seen as an asset, not a threat. I was 50 years old.

I received tenure and promotion to full professor. I continued my work, but objective conditions deteriorated in Canada. In Toronto, this was especially the case with the explosion of poverty, food insecurity and food bank use, and homelessness leading the United Way of Greater Toronto to label the 1990s a "decade of decline". Yet governments, healthcare, and public health agencies for the most part continued to be uninterested in these developments. This was not the case among other sectors of Canadian life. Agencies and organizations involved in addressing poverty, dealing with the homeless, and supplying emergency food to the hungry were cognizant of these developments. The labour movement and various social justice organizations and faith communities could see it. In fact it would appear that just about anyone would make the connection between the deteriorating public policy environment and the health of Canadians. Surely, elected representatives would see the obvious and begin to develop and implement public policies in support of health?

But this was not to be the case. The concerted efforts of the business community to justify the skewing of public policy to their interests, the neoliberal discourse of minimizing government interventions in worship of the unfettered, "free" market, and the increasingly concentrated corporate media's championing of globalization obstructed these views. Canadian institutional response to the potential health effects of these developments became even more warped.

Governments allocated hundreds of millions of dollars to lifestyle messaging which was eagerly snatched up by public health agencies. Even larger amounts were devoted to research designed to combat various "epidemics" (eg obesity, unhealthy eating, sedentary behaviour, etc) identified by de-politicized health authorities and university researchers that served to further obscure the structural changes taking place in Canadian society.

These lifestyle research and public health industries shape media and public understandings of the determinants of health. The result of which is to create a media and general public whose understandings of the negative influence of recent public policy developments—especially those of the regressive type—upon their own and their neighbours' health and well-being is undeveloped to say the least.

Tides of Change?

Despite these disturbing trends in public policy, civil servants at Health Canada laboured away at raising issues of the broader determinants of health. Health Canada provided me with funding to organize a 2002 national conference on the social determinants of health across the lifespan. Over 400 Canadians and two Americans attended the conference. The 1994 volume *Social Determinants of Health: Canadian Perspectives* that resulted from the conference has sold close to 7000 copies and a second edition is now in progress. I established a Social Determinants of Health listserv that currently has 1200 members. Public health units across Canada have now begun to consider ways of addressing broader determinants of health. The Ontario public health community has explicitly urged the province to incorporate economic and social determinants of health into the public health mandate.

In 2006, sensing the urgency of raising these issues among students in the health disciplines, I edited a text that brought together much of the critical work being done on health policy and healthcare in Canada and the USA, *Staying Alive: Critical Perspectives on Health, Illness, and Health Care*. In 2007 I authored *Poverty and Policy in Canada: Implications for Health and Quality of Life*. These books are proving as popular outside of the academic community as within it.

I am on the road a lot. Some of the groups that ask to be educated about the social determinants of health and the political, economic, and social forces that shape these include community development organizations, community health centres, public health units, hospitals, social justice and religious groups, and professional associations associated with social work, legal aid, municipal services, and nursing, among others. Most of my engagements are in Canada, but I have also been invited to Georgia, Kentucky, Maine, Minnesota, Ohio, and Washington State to discuss the American public policy scene and its effects upon health.

In Canada, the Provinces of Quebec and Newfoundland and Labrador have developed plans to reduce the incidence of poverty. In November 2007 the federal Leader of the Opposition (Liberal Party of Canada) announced a pledge—if elected—to reduce the incidence of poverty in Canada by 30% for adults and 50% for children in five years. Similarly, the Premier of Ontario (Liberal Party of Canada) also announced a commitment to *address* poverty. On the negative ledger, the Liberal Party has done little in the past to address these issues so the value of such commitments remains unclear. On the positive ledger, the issue of poverty—and the public policies that can be implemented to reduce its incidence—is being discussed. Comparative research indicates that poverty reduction usually comes about only if social democratic parties of the left achieve power or influence through the presence of legislative minorities in elected chambers. It was with this understanding that I solicited Jack Layton, the leader of the federal New Democratic Party of Canada, to contribute the foreword to *Poverty and Policy in Canada: Implications for Health and Quality of Life*. The struggle continues.

Lessons Learned

What can be learned from all this? First, there are means of integrating political knowledge and passion with academic inquiry. Second, this may not be easy to do. Third, there are ways of simplifying the journey. I provide these in the form of 10 tips—in order of importance—for being a public scholar.

Ten Tips for Being a Public Scholar

1 Be true to yourself and your beliefs. Have no fear.
2 Choose an academic discipline that allows incorporation of the political into academic inquiry.
3 Get research funding.
4 Become a successful teacher.
5 Recognize that communities—especially marginalized ones—are the best authorities on their lives and the factors that influence its quality.
6 Build trust with community organizations and agencies that share your values.
7 Publish and then publish even more.
8 Get tenured.

9 Build networks to provide academic, psychological, and political support to your efforts.

10 Be proactive: interact with the public and recognize that both you and the public have much to offer each other.

It is much easier to carry out these kinds of activities if you have a résumé that indicates you are a "serious scholar". Being such does not assure that you will be free of threat and insecurity for your political-scholarly activities. It may be best to first achieve tenure in your discipline. Then— unless things drastically change for the worse—you now have a free path to carry out—and publicize—critical studies that have some relevance for people's lives. It is a path that is actually relatively easy for most academics to do. It still amazes me that so few actually do it.

References

Dumhoff GW (1967) *Who Rules America?* Englewood Cliffs, NJ: Prentice-Hall.

Harding S (ed) (1987) *Feminism and Methodology: Social Science Issues*. Bloomington: Indiana University Press.

Kerlinger F (1986) *Foundations of Behavioral Research*. New York: Holt, Rinehart and Winston.

Mills CW (1956) *The Power Elite*. New York: Oxford University Press.

Porter J (1965) *The Vertical Mosaic: An Analysis of Social Class and Power in Canada*. Toronto: University of Toronto Press.

Raphael D, Renwick R, Brown I, Phillips S, Sehdev H and Steinmetz B (2001) Community quality of life in low income urban neighbourhoods: Findings from two contrasting communities in Toronto, Canada. *Journal of the Community Development Society* 32(2):310–333.

Tesh S (1990) *Hidden Arguments: Political Ideology and Disease Prevention Policy*. New Brunswick, NJ: Rutgers University Press.

Wilkinson RG (1996) *Unhealthy Societies: The Afflictions of Inequality*. New York: Routledge.

Wilson J (1983) *Social Theory*. Englewood Cliffs, NJ: Prentice Hall.

Suggested Reading

Esping-Andersen G (1985) *Politics against Markets: The Social Democratic Road to Power*. Princeton: Princeton University Press. Esping-Anderson's analysis of how social democracy achieved power in Scandinavia provides various insights into what needs to be done.

Esping-Andersen G (1990) *The Three Worlds of Welfare Capitalism*. Princeton: Princeton University Press. The definitive text that identified how developed welfare states can be defined as social democratic, conservative or liberal political economies. The USA and Canada are liberal political economies.

Esping-Andersen G (1999) *Social Foundations of Post-Industrial Economies*. New York: Oxford University Press. This significant updating of Esping-Andersen's (1990) work incorporates gender and familial analyses into his typology of welfare states.

Hofrichter R (ed) (2003) *Health and Social Justice: A Reader on Politics, Ideology, and Inequity in the Distribution of Disease*. San Francisco: Jossey Bass. The definitive collection of original and previously published articles that address the relationship between social justice and health.

Mills C W (1958/2000) *The Sociological Imagination.* New York: Oxford University Press. As fresh today as when it was written, this volume outlines the key questions that social scientists must address in order to understand society and its problems.

Navarro V (ed) (2002) *The Political Economy of Social Inequalities: Consequences for Health and Quality of Life.* Amityville, NY: Baywood Press.

Navarro V (ed) (2007) *Neoliberalism, Globalization, and Inequalities: Consequences for Health and Quality of Life.* Amityville, NY: Baywood Press.

Navarro V and Muntaner C (eds) (2004) *Political and Economic Determinants of Population Health and Well-being: Controversies and Developments.* Amityville, NY: Baywood Press. These three volumes are collections of important papers on the political economy of health previously published in the International Journal of Health Services.

Raphael D (ed) (2004) *Social Determinants of Health: Canadian Perspectives.* Toronto: Canadian Scholars' Press.

Raphael D (2007) *Poverty and Policy in Canada: Implications for Health and Quality of Life.* Toronto: Canadian Scholars' Press.

Raphael D, Bryant T and Rioux M (eds) (2006) *Staying Alive: Critical Perspectives on Health, Illness, and Health Care.* Toronto: Canadian Scholars' Press. These three volumes provide the latest developments in the determinants of health, the political economy of health and health care, and poverty and public policy. While focused on the Canadian scene, the insights are certainly relevant to the public policy and health care situations in jurisdictions outside Canada.

Tesh S (1990) *Hidden Arguments: Political Ideology and Disease Prevention Policy.* New Brunswick, NJ: Rutgers University Press. Tesh's book is a landmark that exposes the ideology behind the dominant approaches to understanding health and its determinants in North America and elsewhere.

Wilson J (1983) *Social Theory.* Englewood Cliffs NJ: Prentice Hall. *Social Theory* is a most remarkable book that provides an overview of the numerous sociological approaches to understanding society and its social structures. Out of print, it is usually obtainable through used book sellers on the Internet.

Chapter 9

Weaving Solidarity from Oneonta to Oxchuc

Katherine O'Donnell

From Oneonta to Oxchuc, and from skateboarders to Mayan weavers, I have been working with people to address community concerns across the multiple borders of generation, class, culture, and global north and south. I see the central challenge of academics as learning to work cooperatively to construct just, collective responses to the structural problems we all face—using the tools of our trade to facilitate this work. This is the work of public sociology.

Making linkages between theory and practice has been the core of my academic work for nearly three decades. My inspiration comes in part from my Estonian, refugee mother, who tirelessly built community across borders, always remaining respectful of the people and heritages of two countries. My undergraduate organizing with Ralph Nader's Public Interest Research Group (PIRG) also gave me early insights into the crucial links between academic life and the wider community.

In 1980, as a new faculty member at Hartwick College, I worked with students to create a Women's Center and then became the Center's advisor for over a decade. We also formed a local chapter of the National Organization for Women (NOW) and wrote monthly newsletters for area campuses and the community. NOW and the Women's Center collaborated on developing conferences, marches, rallies, and community events. Such collaborations between activists on campus and in the community continued throughout the 1980s and 1990s and emerged in my classes initially as "Praxis Groups". Later they evolved into community-action teams (CATs), which are student team approaches to community-based work and research in major policy areas.

Programs which offer community-based training to students are embedded in and shaped by complex power relations, a principal one being the relationship between the university and the community. Solidarity relationships can challenge this power dynamic. In contrast to charity or entrepreneurial models, which are often used by academics, non-government organizations (NGOs), and others responsible for organizing community and international programs, the notion of a solidarity relationship involves praxis, education for liberation for all parties, and the transformation of oppressive conditions. Solidarity ethics, such as those advocated by Paul Farmer and Vandana Shiva, calls for us to take our cues from the communities with whom we work. Our work must address structural violence—issues reflecting or associated with the root causes of poverty, the unequal access to resources, and the loss of dignity. This approach also demands engaging ourselves in understanding our own locations in the global systems that produce these inequities. Community-based service learning exposes students and faculty to communities that differ from their own by race, age, class, culture, and life experience—and challenges us all to confront racism, class inequality, and privilege worldwide.

Of all the campus-community projects that I have undertaken in the past three decades, my work with the Oneonta Community Alliance for Youth (OCAY) confirms, for me, the importance of grassroots organizing around people's concerns and interests. In 1996, the criminalization of skateboarding youth in my community led to the development of OCAY. The formation of this inter-generational group was in direct response to the demands of parents, young teens, and community members. It also flowed from conversations parents and I had on a bus trip returning from a Stand for Children rally in DC that I organized.

We began by organizing community forums to address youth issues and specifically skateboarding. We lobbied city hall, organized fundraisers, wrote editorials, organized teen music events, and partnered with local groups to build a skateboard park. We were successful, and the park opened locally in 2001. Since 2003, we have been working to re-establish a teen center and a teen after-school program in the city and, in fall 2006, OCAY launched the Oneonta Teen Center in the basement of the former Armory. In the last 2 years, our fund-raising events, including coffeehouses, music shows, Rock & Bowl, and Summerfest, have attracted over 3000 teens and their families and galvanized teen leadership, youth voice, youth talent, and parental, educational, business, civic, arts, and government collaboration. Scores of Hartwick College students have rallied to that cause, as students and researchers.

In the case of OCAY, I utilized community action teams to train students to work in groups with organizations in the community. The community work is linked to specific classes that review relevant sociological literatures and concepts. For example, I developed a course entitled "Teens and families", which covers issues of teens and schools, class, social status, gender, teen risk-taking behaviors, and teen empowerment.

My activist research seeks to understand "life at the border of school" (Fine 2000) where community-based programs and interactions with college students and staff function as alternative spaces for youth identity work. Fine (2000:2) describes such places as "construction sites where youth create, invent, reconstruct, critique, and reassemble identities" and where they "seek meaning, recognition, and comfort".

In order to tap teen interests and concerns to utilize for program development and grants, I recently surveyed over 600 local teens at the junior and senior high schools. The survey itself was developed by me, with feedback from student fieldwork and OCAY teens, and distributed and collected through the high-school sociology course by OCAY teen leaders. Other students conducted interviews with key community people and did newspaper research on the city's past teen programs. Within my courses, students do analytic papers to apply key theoretical concepts to their work in community settings, as mentors, assistants, fundraisers, and program developers. In 2006, my student intern also helped launch the Teen Center programming and completed SPSS analysis of the survey data.

With respect to the early, utopian mission of my college, OCAY represents a strong commitment to education for the common good and to the cultivation of democratic ideals and practices. Accomplishing this entails working on building institutional links, designing integrated curricula, developing faculty buy-in through various reward structures, and communicating effectively with the relevant constituencies, including students and city partners. Civic academic practice is at the nexus of mission and sense of place and informs pedagogy, curriculum, and research. Particular challenges include educating students for the long haul and creating enduring social structures that must live beyond a course, semester, and professor.

Friends of Jolom Mayaetik Transnational Solidarity Network

Creating an economic solidarity relationship with my colleagues in Chiapas, Mexico since 1998 has pushed me to a new level of public scholarship. In this case, work-based educational delegations to Chiapas and the US marketing of Fair Trade textiles made by the 350-person Mayan women's weaving cooperative, *Jolom Mayaetik*, brings me into contact with thousands of people and scores of churches, community centers, elementary and secondary schools, organizations, and universities across the US, Mexico, Europe, and Canada. Framing this intercultural work for diverse audiences has become one of my main jobs and is central to my teaching, public lectures, and grants.

The solidarity network works on generating income, as well as awareness about human rights, indigenous women's leadership, cooperative practice, and our collective role in challenging inequity. Our economic solidarity literally translates into markets for fine textiles and, therefore, into income for the cooperative's members and their families. It also generates opportunities for popular education and squarely locates our lives in the context of the shared impact of global economic apartheid and the security, human rights, and sustainability challenges we all face.

In both cases, the projects emerge from structural issues which are identified and confronted through grassroots efforts. The link to the academy is made possible through interpersonal bridges between folks with strong community ties, creative curricular and department coursework for training and community-based learning, community-based research, and links to college mission.

Linking ourselves and our students to organizations pursuing solidarity relationships north and south focuses attention on structural inequalities, as they manifest themselves in local and global contexts and on the possibility of solidarity networks for change. As public activist scholars, we can foster the sharing and acquisition of such skills through skill-building workshops, alliances, lobbying, community-based research, and alternative development with community members, students, and colleagues. Using our organizations and their resources more strategically to link to existing local, national, and global organizations and struggles is a solidarity and sustainability challenge.

My pedagogy emerges from activist, feminist, Freire-inspired popular education models. In the case of Jolom Mayaetik and our solidarity work, our commitment has entailed learning first hand from our partners about their processes and philosophies—accompaniment, collectivism, and resistance to inequality. Our alignment with the resources and practices of our sister organizations has also meant that in 2002 and again in 2005, we worked with Jolom and K'inal Antzetik on building projects as determined by the organizations in Chiapas. In 2005, our delegation also visited with six communities and in each site spoke with Jolom Mayaetik members and representatives about important issues confronting them, including arranged marriages, domestic violence, land conflicts, lack of potable water, severe economic hardship and poverty, and women's resistance and organizing. Students met with many civil society groups organizing for change.

At the same time that delegations were replacing conventional courses, work in the north took on popular education forms and also moved from campus to community. In 2001, I worked with students to create our first Anti-Sweatshop Fashion Show based on Maquila Solidarity Network's model. This proved to be a great way to involve students in a variety of roles, from researchers, to models, and DJs—all to make the link between student consumption patterns, clothing produced in sweatshops, and fair trade, anti-sweat alternatives.

The Jolom story has also become part of public tours on the theme of "Women Confronting Globalization". These coast-to-coast tours are organized around major academic conferences, where I travel with members of Jolom and K'inal and other US solidarity workers to link with people from churches, schools, weavers' groups, community centers, citizen groups, and colleges across the US. We discuss the effects of globalization, co-operative development, indigenous rights, trade policy, and Mayan weaving. Our workshops, talks, and popular education have also become part of our presentations and sales at the Society for Applied Anthropology Annual Conference, the American Anthropology Association Conference, and the International Folk Art Market in Santa Fe. The Jolom story in global context informs the marketing of their textiles.

In the case of Jolom, the college's emphasis on intercultural experiences and our 40-year tradition of intensive study during January terms creates the institutional spaces necessary for the academic dimension of this partnership. Having students commit to long-term work with Jolom Mayaetik remains a challenge, and the institutional infrastructure and resource sharing needed to support an international partnership are emergent. Formalizing the loosely structured US solidarity network and shifting the relationship from a curricular and, therefore, fleeting experience, to an organization would stimulate more consistent student, institutional, and network involvement, external financial support, a visible US presence, and sustainability for the cooperative.

Participatory Democracy

When I began this work as a junior faculty member, I had strong departmental support, and the tenure committee at Hartwick had a Boyer-based, broad sense of what constituted "scholarly" work. I was lucky. For most young faculty and most institutions, it remains risky to undertake projects like these. Later on, serving as chair of Sociology for 15 years and as coordinator of the Women's Studies program for nine years gave me lots of creative, departmental curricular power. This did not, however, often translate into institutional power regarding the construction of a college community partners program. For me, participatory democracy has meant empowering people and linking campus and community via organizing, programs, curriculum, and local, national, and global projects. We are using our experiences, cross-cultural knowledge, and scholarly frameworks and research to inform our work and analysis and to critically reflect on that same work in the hope of forging community and social justice.

Substantial challenges in the community-based work that I have undertaken include recognizing how power plays out in various settings. For students, challenges include gaining voice, working collaboratively in groups, collectively organizing and challenging in a systematic rather than haphazard way, using research to inform actions, working with the community members and respecting their knowledge and expertise, learning not to expect immediate results, thinking of their work as cumulative, realizing that their academic or personal needs do not always come first, learning to negotiate, compromise, challenge, and lobby, and, most importantly, learning not to give up.

Academic institutions are challenged to be inclusive and to move beyond their often gated culture. The academy can be instrumental in forging new relationships but must honor the community's diverse leaders, history, and structural challenges.

With respect to OCAY and Jolom, the most difficult task remains developing enduring student and institutional commitment. For the academy and community, class interests and power inequities translate into agendas and priorities—thus the transnational solidarity relation is particularly daunting. Potential mechanisms to institutionalize relations include Memoranda of Mutual Understanding, partnerships, centers, institutes, coalitions, social movements, and joint socio-economic projects. In conclusion, there are important lessons to be learned at every level by undertaking community-based work-lessons that include disciplinary specifics, but which extend far beyond to life, social justice, and the practice of democracy.

Suggested Reading

AAC (1991) *The Challenge of Connecting Learning*. Washington, DC.

Boyer E (1990) *Scholarship Reconsidered: Priorities of the Professoriate*. Princeton, NJ: Carnegie Foundation for the Advancement of Teaching.

Farmer P (2004) *Pathologies of Power-Health, Human Rights, and the New War on the Poor*. Berkeley: University of California Press.

Fine M (2000) *Construction Sites—Excavating Race, Class, and Gender among Urban Youth*. New York: Teachers College Press.

Fraser N (1989) *Unruly Practices: Power, Discourse, and Gender in Contemporary Theory*. St Paul: University of Minnesota Press.

Freire P (1989) *Pedagogy of the Oppressed*. New York: Continuum Press.

Shiva V and Meis M (1993) *Ecofeminism*. London: Zed Books.

Chapter 10

Demand the Possible: Journeys in Changing our World as a Public Activist-Scholar

Paul Chatterton

Sometimes I wonder why I work in a university at all. I spend most of my time outside of it, organising community events, helping out at a local free space, supporting local co-ops, doing asylum seeker support, going to activist gatherings and demonstrations, helping with campaigns, putting on film screenings, and hosting radical speakers. I suppose I have become someone who blends activism and the academy. As a result, life is busy, challenging, confusing, but generally enjoyable.

Then I remember why I still work in a university. It's because I'm an activist-scholar, someone who sees the value in radical education and the public debate of ideas which challenge the norm. I bring my activism into the university for a number of reasons. In spite of the way they are being re-engineered, universities are still amazing places of encounter, conflict, diversity and debate (not to mention resources), and it is crucial that we find ways to defend and expand these and open them up to others. Engaging with the activist world, while it raises the eyebrows of many senior colleagues, excites and inspires my students. It reminds me of what Paulo Freire once said about the purpose of education: it is the practice of freedom. Defending education as a path to freedom and not as a route to debt, precarious jobs, and conformity is one of the most important political tasks of our time. And it's also an essential antidote to the endless consumer parade which student life has become, as well as to the efforts of British Aerospace, KPMG, Deloitte, and their ilk, to parcel up their futures.

So how does all this work? What does it mean to be an activist-scholar? How do you promote radical ideas and debates within the academy? I want to explain through three stories: my involvement in challenging the publishing giant Elsevier, the formation of a new Masters programme called "Activism and Social Change", and my work with a popular education collective called Trapese.

Take One: Disarm Dsei: Arm your Writing

September 11, 2001. You will remember it for the obvious reasons. But I remember it because I was dressed in a large pink cardboard tank outside the biannual Defence Systems Exhibition International (DSEI) arms fair at London's ExCel centre. I was there as part of the DisarmDsei mobilisations which were taking direct action against one of the world's largest arms fairs. It wasn't until May 2006, however, after talking with Dave Featherstone from Liverpool University, and friends from the Campaign against the Arms Trade (CAAT), that I became aware that publishing giant Reed Elsevier (RE) was involved in organising DSEI through a subsidiary of the Reed Group, Reed Exhibitions. Our initial reaction was "what the hell are academic publishers doing in the arms trade!" Reed Elsevier publishes many of the key journals in the discipline of Geography. We decided that the links were obvious and serious and we had to highlight this by writing a piece in the journal *Political Geography* calling for a boycott of RE journals.

We submitted an article to *Political Geography* entitled "Elsevier, Critical Geography and the arms trade", which appeared in 2007. In the article we pointed out that at the London arms fair, which RE had organized, around 1000 exhibitors sell everything from battleships and attack helicopters to cluster bombs and machine guns. We noted that this represented a significant "disconnect" between the types of research and ideas promoted most frequently in the journal, and the actual practices of the journal's publisher. We wrote:

> This situation represents a challenge to the geographical community. Are we as critical, left leaning academics willing to accept a situation whereby some of the most significant journals in the discipline are owned by a company which aggressively promotes the arms trade? ... This does not seem to us an acceptable situation. Beyond this Editorial/Intervention we therefore will refuse to publish in Elsevier publications or to referee papers for Elsevier journals until the company divests itself of links to the arms trade. As such a divesture is unlikely, one option may be for these journals to find friendlier homes in the publishing world. We are also calling for the wider geographical community to take action against this situation.

The next issue featured an anonymous response from an RE spokesperson, who attempted to defend the company's involvement in the arms trade by arguing that not just the military, but also equipment for peaceful and defensive uses was traded at the fair.

The debate didn't end there. It quickly emerged that RE was publishing an important book in Geography, *The International Encyclopaedia of Human Geography*. Hundreds of geographers had been asked to contribute entries for this encyclopaedia, and as the links between RE and the arms trade spread, people began to withdraw their entries. There was a long debate amongst the editors about the ethical issues surrounding the project, but in March 2007, the senior editors issued a statement explaining why they would continue the project with RE. Their argument was threefold: first they argued that since we are compromised in nearly every area of our lives in everything we do, why is their project and this company being highlighted? Second, people had already invested time in the project; third, the editors had to honour commitments already made.

These reasons rang hollow to us. Like the Elsevier spokesperson's reaction, they represent a classic (non)response to challenges to the status quo of our everyday worklives. None of the editors' reasons explained why the project could not go ahead without RE, using for example, increasingly common open source publishing models such as Creative Commons Licenses or wiki pages for the on-line version. Wouldn't this then make it a truly public and free project like it should have been in the first place?

Even though the encyclopedia project continues with RE, the controversy around it reached the public domain, and in 2007 RE decided to pull out of the arms fair business. This has given countless geographers hope that we can act collectively and effectively as an academic community. The key point of being a critical geographer, for me, is to connect with wider public debates on injustice, inequality and oppression, especially those we find in our daily working lives. Small victories like these are essential to motivate people to further action. There remain thousands of Reed Elseviers out there in our work worlds, but we are now learning how to challenge them publicly.

Take Two: Radicalise Learning

Being a public scholar is not just about being "out there" beyond the walls of the university. It is also about radicalising our own workplaces and teaching. To these ends, I have developed a new Masters programme called "Activism and Social Change" in the School of Geography at the University of Leeds. This programme is unlike many academic courses. It is infused with ideas about the possibilities of more horizontal social organisation, and the abilities of people to manage their own affairs through mutual aid and solidarity. It presents a commitment to workable alternatives to the daily grind of wage labour and monetary exchange, and a mistrust of those with blueprints or vanguardist leadership.

I wanted to develop a course that would introduce students to these ideas, not in a doctrinaire or theoretical way, but as living ideas that would catch their imagination and act as possible openings for how we might live more sustainable, just and equal lives. The really tough question we asked in the class was "what do we mean by 'activism'"? Activism takes many forms, and visions of social change differ across time and space. Business activists, for example, have been the most successful activists of recent years. We did not want to fix ourselves to one particular ideological or political viewpoint—we certainly aren't all Marxists or anarchists. But we do see ourselves and our visions for social change as part of what has become known as the "anti-capitalist", "anti-globalisation" or "global justice" movement, which has become visible at the summit sieges of Seattle, Prague and Cancun, and the World Social Forums.

We have come under fire from many activists and campaigners who see us professionalising something that should be organic and on the streets. However, we have responded by saying that our energy will come from breaking down barriers between the university and broader social movements for change, and courses such as these are the first step. In terms of content, we have developed modules in radical ideas, resistance movements, skills for researching and campaigning on social change, engagements with activists and campaigners, how to implement ideas, and a large action-research dissertation. Campaign groups such as the World Development Movement, Friends of the Earth, and CorporateWatch have officially backed the course because it engages the outside world and builds skills for campaigning and action. In a situation where alternative ideas are marginalised and social movements are often repressed, there simply needs to be more of these kinds of radical education projects to help build and support campaigning and social movements. They also reclaim space within universities from depoliticised, or at least corporate-focused, education and career options. We need to create, expand, and defend these forms of radical education.

Take Three: Make the Leap

I've spent a lot of time outside the walls of academia with a popular education collective called Trapese (Taking Radical Action through Popular Education and Sustainable Everything!). Many people were upset to find out that we were not circus trapese performers! Our motto "making the leap" refers instead to ideas and action and not the high wire. In 2004, the Collective started developing workshops in the build-up to the 2005 summit of the Group of 8 Nations, which was being held in Gleneagles, Scotland. We toured the UK, and Europe giving workshops on the role of the G8, and the big issues on the agenda such as climate change and debt, with student unions, church groups, and peace and campaign groups. Our focus concerned understanding what the G8 meant, as an elite group of nations who set the global agenda for the maintenance of the capitalist economy, and also discussing what workable alternatives existed to give people a sense that other worlds and ways of living are possible beyond those proposed by the G8. Here we introduced examples such as community gardens, workers co-operatives, and social movements such as the Zapatistas, union organisers and campaigns on climate change. We also focused on action planning and how people could empower themselves to take action both in terms of joining the protests against the G8 and also developing local campaigns afterwards.

Since then, we have developed a range of workshops and skill-sharing sessions. We found a huge demand for workshops which focused not just on the issues, but also what skills and abilities people needed to engage with the issues. We have worked with a number of groups such as the Permaculture Association which gives courses on the principles of permaculture design; Seeds for Change which gives workshops on facilitation, consensus decision making and direct democracy; alternative media groups such as Indymedia and ClearerChannel who actively promote and help distribute alternative media and film as tools of empowerment; members of the UK social centres network who actively encourage occupied and self-managed social centres; direct action collectives who develop tactics for taking action and campaigning; and cultural activists such as the Clandestine Rebel Clown Army and the Vacuum Cleaner who bring together art and activism to pull stunts, occupy offices and make interventions (including my favourite, Praying for Products, which involves a large group of people kneeling down in front of a well known branded item and numerous bemused shoppers in a large chain store, and giving thanks at the top of your voice to the world of consumer goods!).

Working alongside these activist-oriented associations inspired us to create a handbook to empower people to get involved in social change. In the end, the book was called, *Do It Yourself, a Handbook for Changing our World*, which was edited by the Trapese Collective and published by Pluto Press in 2007. The intention of the book was to blend ideas with a practical "how to" guide. The topics we covered included sustainable living, decision making, education, health, food, cultural activism, media, direct action and free spaces. The crucial part of this project for us was that the reader could learn about the issues and then see practical advice on how you could instantly implement ideas. So, for example, a discussion about the impacts of peak oil and the end of cheap energy was complemented by a guide to build a solar shower in your back garden. We insisted that the book was published under a creative commons license that allows people to use the material freely for non-commercial uses, and it was collectively written to move away from individual names and reputations. These are small additions, but they really change the feel of the work we produce.

So what did we achieve by writing this book? Most importantly, we want education to inspire others to get involved in change. We have to address apathy, denial, powerlessness and often just a lack of time. This is easily done through templates for action, action planning, inspiring stories and crucial emotional support. My work with Trapese aims to take to the public discussions on big issues such as privatization, climate change, resource conflict, social inequalities, and political apathy, whilst at the same time talking about what kinds of workable alternatives are feasible. These issues are too important to lock up in small academic seminars and inaccessible journal articles.

Be Realistic, Demand the Impossible. . .

Let's save our pessimism for better times. These are my stories of being a public scholar-activist, of challenging, inspiring and innovating in my work and life. I want to galvanize dissent, normalize critique, and make radical alternatives seem like real possibilities for our times. There are always possibilities for radicalising public debates, be they in our workplaces (disputes with management, supporting junior members of staff, challenging corporate restructuring and management diktats, introducing radical ideas into our teaching) or outside (helping groups with campaign strategies, showing solidarity to those in resistance, attending events and demonstrations, lobbying and defending for particular causes). The progressive Left is weak in its ability to justify, demand and argue publicly for the implementation of our utopias— be they co-operative working practices, less work, more pay, or the safeguarding of public goods and services. Critical Geography has a role to play in voicing these real dreams and desires and creating public debates around them. Our job is to make alternatives seem feasible and sensible, not crazy and left field. It is a battle of ideas, words and practices about a better world, a battle, alas, that too many professors forget once they have joined the elite club. Here's a few things we can all do:

- Introduce as much challenging material into our teaching as possible—including street work, innovative assessment, learning radical histories, outside engagements.
- Push for new courses in universities which actively promote engagement, campaigning and civic activism.
- Support open source and online publishing and challenge metrics.
- Inform ourselves about who owns the journals and books we publish in. Which large firms are behind them? Support the ones we feel comfortable with and tell those we avoid why.
- Spread the word on corporations who have too much influence in our work lives and get together with others to challenge them.
- Try and create publicly accessible versions of our work in the form of pamphlets, tip sheets or websites.

Life's too short. Push the boundaries, kick up a fuss, organise with friends. Don't let management push you around! Challenge lazy, overpaid professors, connect with inspiring movements for change, and turn your work places into spaces of joy, hope and rebellion!

Online Resources

Campaign Against the Arms Trade. Campaign group against militarization, http://www.caat.org Accessed 4 February 2008.

Clandestine Insurgent Rebel Clown Army. How to take direct action through rebel clowning, http://www.clownarmy.org Accessed 4 February 2008.

ClearerChannel. Group promoting grassroots media and activism, http://www.cleaerchannel.org Accessed 4 February 2008.

Creative Commons Licenses. All you need to know about going copyleft, http://www.creativecommons.org Accessed 4 February 2008.

DisArm DSEI campaign site, http://www.dsei.org, Accessed 4 February 2008.

Indymedia. News from the streets from around the world, http://www.indymedia.org Accessed 4 February 2008.

Kiptik Zapatista Solidarity Group, http://www.kiptik.buz.org Accessed 4 February 2008.

MA in Activism and Social Change at the University of Leeds, http://www.activismsocialchange.org.uk Accessed 4 February 2008.

Permaculture Association. Lots of information about this inspiring design strategy for changing our world, http://www.permaculture.org.uk Accessed 4 February 2008.

Seeds for Change Collective who undertake workshops on consensus and direct democracy, http://www.seedsforchange.org Accessed 4 February 2008.

The Common Place, Leeds' autonomous social centre in the UK, http://www.thecommonplace.org.uk Accessed 4 February 2008.

The Vacuum Cleaner. Hilarious, effective and inspiring creative direct action outfit, http://www.thevacuumcleaner.org Accessed 4 February 2008.

Tom Stafford's on line petition, http://www.idiolect.org.uk/elsevier/petition.php Accessed 4 February 2008.

Trapese Popular Education Collective. Resources for popular education, http://www.trapese.org Accessed 4 February 2008.

Trapese Popular Education Collective. *Do it Yourself: A Handbook for Changing Our World*. London: Pluto Press, http://www.handbookforchange.org Accessed 4 February 2008.

Wikipedia on line resource, http://www.wikipedia.org Accessed 4 February 2008.

Chapter 11

Becoming a Scholar-Advocate: Participatory Research with Children

Meghan Cope

Passionate Trajectories

I have long felt for myself, and have advised my students, that the best scholarship comes from the heart and has the potential to resonate broadly around an important problem. In part, finding one's niche based on one's true interests is important for sustaining the energy and commitment that are needed for long-term projects. I believe this forms the foundations of good public scholarship because issues we care deeply about are the ones for which we make extra efforts to reach out, disseminate, and advocate. However, there are always challenges along the way because much of our research—especially that involving participatory types of ethnography—involves slow, steady, often mundane tasks and it can be hard to keep our eyes on the bigger picture.

My own graduate work in urban geography was historical and generated a certain frustration for me in that I felt I could do little to make my subjects' lives *better*; after all, they had already passed away. While there are certain comforts in researching the past, and there are rich traditions of public scholarship based on historical work (cf Patricia Limerick's contribution to this volume), when I started my first tenure-track job I made a strategic decision that I would take a break from dusty archives. I wanted to work with real, live people and I hoped that my research would have a direct impact on people's lives. I had rosy visions of becoming a scholar whose sensitive and revelatory fieldwork with marginalized social groups would quickly cause policy to shift, lift the burdens of poverty, sexism, and racism, and facilitate new means of empowerment. Needless to say, things haven't worked out that way (at least so far!), but in many ways my youthful optimism and ignorance served me well. If I had known then about how intransigent the forces of oppression are I may never have started along the path I am still traveling. As part of this, I have come to see that public scholarship need not necessarily be about large-scale or rapid social change. I have come to appreciate the value of listening to people, and of the small, incremental steps that may take years to lead to something more, but that often lead to something better.

Several years into my first job, I finally took my own advice and turned to a longstanding interest in two topics—cities and children. I combined these passions in a proposal that was funded by the NSF (*mirabile dictu!*) and many years later I still love the topic and am learning new things every day. The Children's Urban Geographies project ultimately looks very little like what I imagined at first (in part because of the difference between starry-eyed envisioning and the actual material and personal realities of research), but in countless ways I think it has turned out *better*. Reflecting on this project and its spin-offs allows me to identify points of progress (and many challenges) towards public scholarship and advocacy, and also to consider the meanings of "scholar-advocate" that resonate most strongly.

The Children's Urban Geographies Project

One could say that there are some commonalities between cities and children. They are both complicated and contradictory. They are messy, but also fascinating and surprising and lovable. We constantly try to analyze them and understand them while also recognizing that these goals are impossible. And both cities and children simultaneously embody the cumulative past of human endeavors, while representing our best attempts at creating new futures. There is always a risk of romanticizing cities and children, taking their quirks and misdeeds as symbolic of their fundamental complexity. So a project built around how children conceptualize their city and urban spaces within it, as well as how the city incorporates, accommodates, ignores, or even harms its younger residents, is fraught with potential scholarly pitfalls, as well as opportunities.

The Children's Urban Geographies project (ChUG) began with a CAREER award from the National Science Foundation in 2000, part of a program intended to fund junior scholars in work that combined research with innovative teaching and public service. The original goals for ChUG included filling a perceived gap in the urban geography literature by discovering how children conceptualize urban space. But there were also practical considerations such as testing new participatory research methods, creating a service-learning course for university students to get involved with an after-school program, exposing low-income children of color to the field and practice of geography (especially to get beyond memorization-based school versions of the discipline), strengthening relations between the university and the local community, and creating on-line activity plans based on participatory research.

These goals have been achieved for the most part, though it is impossible for me to know the impacts of some of our activities. For example, did we make enough of an impression on any of the children to lead them into a career in geography or urban studies? This is an important question for public scholars: unlike "regular" academia, with its citation indices and impact factors, the effects and outcomes of much of what we do involving "the public" as research subjects, local communities, non-profit organizations, etc, are often untraceable and unknowable. Just when I wonder if I spent five years throwing my efforts down the drain, I receive some little gem of feedback that suggests that those efforts indeed had some kind of impact after all—a postcard from a former student thanking me for changing the way she sees things, a call from a community member who saw a newspaper article about my work and wants to know how to make his town more child friendly, an inquiry from an organization in Buffalo, NY looking for suggestions on getting youth involved in their tree-planting efforts, and so on. Thank goodness for these small tokens, for they truly sustain me!

One of the implicit goals of ChUG was to construct a project with children that was *not* concerned with educating or socializing them, but rather, with listening to and learning from them. I felt from the start that kids living in the neighborhoods of Buffalo surrounding my research site knew far more than I about their city streets, blocks, and the hidden sub-texts of the social landscape. This feeling meshed well with theoretical trends in the "new social studies of childhood", in which child-centered research is highly valued. Being both a mother and a professor, one of my greatest challenges in the project was the struggle to move away from the constant "teaching moments" and didactic mode of interacting with children that comes to me most naturally. I had to force myself to put the participants' interests, views, and ideas at the center. The second greatest challenge was getting university students to think this way too.

This shift in perspective was also representative of a larger move towards becoming a more careful researcher and a better advocate for children's interests and needs with respect to their urban neighborhoods. I see this development as critical to a more nuanced meaning of public scholarship, which rests firmly on the traditions and principles of feminist research and epistemologies. When most Americans think of who constitutes "the public", they probably don't include poor, urban, Hispanic and African–American children. By bracketing my adultist agenda and being critically reflective of my own position with the children in the project, I was creating an opportunity for this multiply oppressed social group to *become* "the public". As they became "the public", I became a public scholar—the two processes were mutually constitutive. In this way, actively receiving the wisdom and knowledge of the children about their urban spaces allowed me to be of service to them, in part by legitimating their ideas as worthy of attention.

I became a public scholar through this process in the sense that I not only listened to an often-silenced group, but I began to serve as their interlocutor in both formal and informal ways. I cannot speak *for* the children involved in the project but I can *speak up* for them. While I feel uncomfortable about stepping into this self-appointed (though hard-earned) position, I also feel that there are so few voices for children with respect to issues such as public space and neighborhoods that they need me. And further, although I cannot truly represent the children who shared their ideas and thoughts with me, as a feminist academic and an ethnographer I *can* identify commonalities, see patterns and understand their underlying processes, and put children's views into a larger picture that has a potentially broader impact. In these ways I consider myself and the ChUG project to be examples of a variety of homegrown public scholarship.

In many ways the ChUG project reflects my feminism too, though we did only limited gender-focused work in the everyday practice of the project. I have always taken feminism to mean the active resistance to oppression on the basis of unequal power relations of many varieties (not just gender) because power relations are so deeply inter-woven. So, my commitment to participatory research inherently demanded that I bracket my own positions in order to listen adequately, while simultaneously recognizing that my interpretations were always saturated with my positions as adult, white, educated, middle-class, suburban, etc; this is a trick feminists have long struggled over with varying degrees of success. This also demanded a certain level of reflexivity in the project—I had to maintain a critical edge to consider the ways my own assumptions and knowledge were shaping the research practice and results—and here the involvement of student researchers who were engaged in the service-learning component of the project was absolutely essential. They kept me honest through their own first encounters with scholarly critical self-reflection, even as I taught them to listen better and focus on the process rather than the product of research. Feminist thought and epistemology have also informed the ways that I considered sharing the results of my work: at first I felt paralyzed by my inability to be the voice of the children, and finding my way through that quandary set the stage for my emerging position as scholar-advocate. Later, however, I discovered some techniques for speaking up for the children that rested more comfortably with my feminist concerns.

Risks and Strategies

I have come to recognize that despite being quite willing to subject my research and teaching to frequent critique, evaluation, and peer review, I may be too thin-skinned to achieve much stature in the media-driven realm of public scholarship. My nascent excursions into publicity—particularly through the printed media—on behalf of making cities better for young people have resulted in a mix of gratifying nods of approval, frustrating misunderstandings (which are difficult to correct), and discouraging criticism. My personal commitments and passion for this subject may sustain my energy and excitement, but they also open my soul to the devastating realization that many people are not convinced by my evidence, nor do they agree with my arguments. My arguments that youth-centered perspectives would help cities be more "livable" for all sorts of social groups are often met with righteous reactions against loud toddlers, youth gangs, or public breastfeeding (which, of course, is not the point I'm making at all). Perhaps I do not have enough of the politician, salesperson, or preacher in me to have cultivated the required single-minded marketing of the idea. Or perhaps I lack the impervious shell of conviction needed to survive public scrutiny. I find that I am fundamentally unprepared for controversy. Am I, then, a failed public scholar?

Early in the ChUG project I held the university's press office at bay because I was still finding my way towards listening to children. I couldn't comfortably present what they had to say when I hadn't even heard it yet. Similarly, I did not want TV cameras accompanying us on our neighborhood field explorations because I felt they would turn our patiently built, delicate sense of trust and respect with the children into a public spectacle over which I had no control. Later in the project I felt more confident that I was fairly representing what the children told and showed me, but I still did not like the loss of control one experiences with the popular press. Not only was I nervous about misrepresenting the children's ideas, I was also leery of critical feedback from the adult public. The passion and heart-felt interest that brought me to the topic of children and cities also made potential criticism sting that much more sharply.

My strategy for coping with these fears rested on a self-constructed legitimacy. First, I drew on the power of naming, and started calling myself the "Director" of the Children's Urban Geographies project. This had more authority to the people in the Mayor's office, government agencies, non-profit organizations, and even other academic units than merely being a professor doing research. This process of naming myself and the project was not wholly disingenuous. I was the principal investigator of the grant and the project had between two and twelve students working on it at any given moment over the course of four years. But it was a strategy that did not immediately occur to me. As a feminist researcher working with marginalized groups and with participatory methods, I had always been reluctant to construct hierarchies. Nevertheless I came to see that the very power I usually resisted could also work in my favor and help me gain both legitimacy and the ear of public authorities. So I found that, regardless of whether I choose to invoke it or not, I do have a certain amount of legitimacy and power through my position as a professor at a university. Despite my anti-hegemonic leanings, this power can be usefully employed in the service of speaking up for children and to that end I am quite happy to trot out whatever credentials might sway the policy wonk, developer, journalist, or program director sitting across the table from me. The goal here is not "publicity" so much as a thoughtful engagement with politicians and others who actually make decisions about the neighborhood conditions real children face every day. This, in turn, aided me in broadcasting the project's results.

The second method I learned was to create reports and brochures (in consultation with the children) with catchy titles and print them in full color on glossy paper, then send them out with a personalized note on university letterhead. The brochures are backed up with websites in which the report is available as a pdf document, and with slideshows and live links to other resources.[1] This strategy helped me to maintain a sense of being "true" to the research but also to share my findings widely. In terms of establishing legitimacy in this realm, a glossy report can be just as—if not more—valuable as a "human interest" clip on the local news station or an op-ed in the daily newspaper. Desktop publishing, cheap ink cartridges, and the internet greatly facilitate this practice, and although I rarely hear back from the recipients of my reports, I know how the public sector works and have at least *some* faith in the slow, incremental effect of my reports' presence on the desks or shelves of multiple agencies.

Thus, at the heart of my participatory research there is also an element of passionate action that goes beyond the potential for chipping away at mundane policies to get at the much bigger issues of the structurally perpetuated deterioration of urban neighborhoods children live in; the intersections of race, class, gender, and youth that create overwhelming situations of oppression; and, ultimately, children's exclusion from "the public" through a series of disempowerments and the pervasive devaluing of children's agency and knowledge. Conveying these messages, however, will continue to be complicated and challenging.

Concluding Thoughts

The most significant shift for me as a scholar over the course of 15 years has been towards participatory, process-oriented research. This has many strengths but also many hurdles with regard to communicating with the adult public. On one hand, participatory research has made me feel more confident about what I know about children and cities because I have learned to listen and observe much better. On the other hand, by letting go of constantly worrying about the material products or outcomes of the project, I have also lost some of the usual types of results and findings that can be used as tools for public scholarship and advocacy. So, while I cannot provide a sound bite for the media on what percentage of children are scared of people in their neighborhoods (I never interviewed or surveyed my participants in such ways), I can weave together multiple conversations, drawings, journal entries, and photos to develop an action list for ways to improve a city street or park that are solidly based on kids' own ideas and dreams, elicited without reference to adult priorities or worldviews. Thus, although we certainly need "hard" data in many instances, and scholars play important roles in informing society about itself through such data, there is also a need for a careful understanding of marginalized groups' perspectives and knowledge. Only with this understanding can we *speak up* for them, at least until the time that they too are recognized as a legitimate "public" worthy of a voice.

Finally, and coming back to feminist concerns regarding positionality and power, I struggle with the question of heroism. In my most honest moments I know that my passionate wish for children to live in *good* cities and for their views to be taken seriously is accompanied by a wish that *I* could be a transformative hero, that something *I* do or write will be the critical factor in making a widespread, meaningful difference. While I would be glad to see substantive change in the lives of urban kids, would I be that much gladder if it was because of something I did? Yes! I do want to be a hero, but what does that say about my own instrumentalist goals, then? Do I embark on such research for the lines on my CV, possible pay raises, and greater glory? To be frank, I *do*, which is a not very comfortable admission. But perhaps this is part of the qualifications for public intellectuals, for scholar-advocates—if we care and are passionate enough about issues to make these many efforts, perhaps we need a little hope that we will also serve as heroes for the cause, as leaders of transformation, and as advocates and champions for the silenced and excluded groups in our society. And this is probably not something to be ashamed of.

Endnote

[1] For example, see http://www.geog.buffalo.edu/research/geokids/, in particular the "LOOP report", aka "The Lots Of Opportunity Project: Empowering children's visions for neighborhood spaces" in which children's ideas for what to do with vacant lots in their area are explored and explained.

Suggested Reading

Here are four books that helped me understand that engaging with many "publics" is both fruitful and fretful.

Chawla L (2002) *Growing Up in an Urbanising World*. Paris: UNESCO/Earthscan.
Freire P (2005 [1970]) *Pedagogy of the Oppressed*. New York: Continuum.
Hart R (1997) *Children's Participation: The Theory and Practice of Involving Young Citizens in Community Development and environmental Care*. New York: UNICEF.
hooks b (2003) *Teaching Community: A Pedagogy of Hope*. New York: Routledge.

Chapter 12

Why Am I Engaged?

Walden Bello

I am often asked this question. It's the sort of question that stops you in your tracks and gets you back to the fundamentals.

Some of my writing as an undergraduate was on economic and social issues but I was more into literature and philosophy, which I loved. I was a late bloomer as an activist. I was pretty much a nose-to-the-grindstone student in college in the Philippines in the mid 1960s. It was only when I went to the States for graduate work in the 1970s that I became an activist owing to the impact of the Vietnam War. I dug into sociology and did my comprehensives even as I got more and more engaged in anti-war protests at Princeton.

My first arrest was a milestone personally. You know, I was in the US as a foreign student, and they had pretty strong rules then against foreign students becoming engaged in political activities. Definitely, if you were arrested for protesting and convicted, you were sent home. During the American foray into Laos in 1971, there was a blockade of the Institute for Defense Analysis on campus. I went to show support for those engaged in civil disobedience, but when I saw how the police were manhandling the protesters, I spontaneously joined them and was arrested and later convicted for trespassing and resisting arrest. I fully expected to be deported but wasn't. But I had crossed a psychological line.

I went to do my dissertation on political organizing in the shantytowns in Chile during the Allende government in 1972. I spent about three months in several urban slums ringing the urban capital, Santiago, when I realized that it was no longer the revolution that was on the ascendant but the counterrevolution. I was intrigued by the dynamics of the counterrevolution at that same time that I felt that what I would gather from studying it would be useful to the left, which I certainly felt myself part of. So I shifted my thesis topic from shantytown organizing to the rise of the counterrevolution and started interviewing elite and middle class folks that were rabid anti-Allendistas. I of course passed myself off as a Princeton researcher, but many of those I talked to could not conceive of a brown-skinned person being in Chile except as a Cuban agent of Fidel Castro, and I narrowly escaped being beaten twice.

I felt though that while one was engaged politically, as an intellectual one had to respect social reality and not distort it for short-term partisan purposes. If the counterrevolution was winning, it was all the more important to understand why the middle classes in particular were being swept up in it. The thesis ended up as a comparative analysis of the rise of counterrevolutionary movements in Chile, Italy in the early 1920s, and Germany in the late 1920s and early 1930s. I wrote it up while I was engaged in solidarity work for Chile in the US.

I guess there were two lessons I drew from my study of the Chilean tragedy. First, that the Pinochet counterrevolution rested on a solid class alliance between the elites and the middle class and that it was not something that was mainly brought about by external intervention from the US, though CIA support for the right was an important element in the triumph of the right. Second, that nothing is more scary than a middle class that is mobilized in the service of the counterrevolution, and from then on I was always skeptical of theories about the middle class being the indispensable pillar of democracy. When the lower classes explode on the political scene as revolutionary actors, the middle class becomes a bastion of the counterrevolution. That happened in Italy, Germany, Spain, and it happened again in Allende's Chile.

The declaration of martial law in the Philippines in 1972 found me in Chile. When I got back to the US, I immediately plunged into exile politics. Since Washington was the key supporter of Marcos, the US became a very strategic area to organize in. So even as I was finishing my thesis, I was shuttling between Princeton and Washington, DC, helping set up what would become a determined lobby seeking a congressional cutoff of military and economic aid to Marcos. A study I co-wrote with Severina Rivera, "The logistics of repression: US aid to the military dictatorship in the Philippines", which came out in 1977, laid out the different channels of US support for the Marcos regime.

While in Washington, I noticed that the greater part of economic aid to Marcos was not going through bilateral channels but through the World Bank. However, World Bank operations in the Philippines were very non-transparent. When you tried to figure out what this giant institution was up to, all you got were sanitized press releases. So to find out what the Bank was doing, we had to break into the Bank to steal documents. This we did over a period of three years, hitting the Bank on those days when nobody was around, like Thanksgiving Day and Christmas Day. We posed as tired Bank staff coming back from missions, with ties askew, and as we fumbled for our "IDs", the guards would just say, don't worry, and wave us through. In the end, we got 3000 pages worth of confidential documents on every Bank project in the country as well as political risk analysis showing the Bank was getting nervous about the opposition to Marcos. The book *Development Debacle: the World Bank in the Philippines* came out in 1982. It became an underground bestseller in the Philippines and people tell me that it was one of the books that mobilized the middle class against Marcos. One lesson I learned from this episode was that to really do good research, you sometimes have to break the law. Had we been caught, my colleagues and I could have gotten 25 years for theft. In fact, the story of how we really got secret Bank documents had to wait until way after the statute of limitations for criminal offenses had passed.

While in the US, I joined the Communist Party of the Philippines (CPP) and spent the next few years going to where I was assigned and doing what the party thought was necessary. I became a full-time activist upon completing my PhD thesis in 1975 and would not return to academia for the next 19 years. For many young Filipinos, to effectively fight the dictatorship in the 1970s and 1980s meant joining the CPP, which was then the most effective resistance organization. It was inspiring, and even as it was disciplined, it was flexible and innovative. It listened to my analysis of things, while at the same time imparting organizational skills to me. Under party guidance, I helped to organize the work in Washington, create the nationwide anti-martial law coalition, set up an international solidarity network, and became a specialist in civil disobedience, taking over consulates and embassies of the Marcos government. The most memorable of these actions was in 1978, when I led a team that occupied the Philippine Consulate in San Francisco for five hours. We were evicted by a SWAT team, arrested, and eventually spent time in jail, from which we got out only after engaging in a one-week-long hunger strike.

I left the party in the late 1980s, after 14 years as a member. Why? In the mid 1980s, it carried out several purges to clean the ranks of suspected military informers. The campaigns eventually took over 2000 lives. I was shocked and decided to investigate what happened. Interviews with scores of people who had participated in these purges either as victims or executioners revealed to me not only the appalling lack of a sound system of justice in the party but also the problem with an outlook that values people only for their class position and politics. Once you were labeled a counterrevolutionary, you were the enemy, subject to whatever punishment the "people" deemed fit for you.

The purges marked the degeneration of what was once a flexible and innovative party into a doctrinal, Stalinist machine. It was heart-rending, seeing this organization degenerate into the same leftist authoritarianism that had not only strangled revolutionary creativity but also begun wiping out its own people along with huge numbers of ordinary citizens in the Soviet Union, China, and Cambodia. The party never forgave me for publicly coming out with my study of the purges. In 2005, I was labeled a "counterrevolutionary" and put on a list of 14 people, some of whom had already been assassinated by the party-led New People's Army.

In 1987, I joined Food First or the Institute for Food and Development Policy in San Francisco, which had been founded in 1975 by Frances Moore Lappe and Joe Collins. This was a time when the newly industrializing countries (NICs) were the flavor of the month, and developing countries were being told to follow the path of the East Asian "tiger economies". It was, in my view, a model that needed to be demystified. In 1990, I and Stephanie Rosenfeld came out with *Dragons in Distress: Asia's Miracle Economies in Crisis*, which was a comprehensive critique of the NIC model. When the Asian financial crisis took place in 1997, it was said that I had anticipated the crisis in *Dragons* by six years. Well, not quite. I detailed an unfolding crisis of economic structure along with crises in the environment and agriculture but I had not foreseen the crisis that would erupt in the financial sphere. The message of the book was that while the NICs had achieved a reduction in the number of people living in poverty and had brought about comprehensive industrialization, export-oriented industrialization was unsustainable and was not a model for other developing countries. The full implications of this message are finally being drawn out these days, when export-oriented development strategies are everywhere in crisis.

After leaving Food First in 1993, I joined the University of the Philippines as a professor of sociology. Nearly 20 years after I got my PhD, I was back in the academy. At the same time, Kamal Malhotra and I set up Focus on the Global South in Bangkok. Focus was meant to be an Asia-based research, advocacy, and action organization working on north–south issues in the age of globalization. We founded Focus in 1995, the same year the World Trade Organization was established, and almost immediately we positioned ourselves against this institution that was designed to be the lynchpin of the system of global governance and against the doctrine of neoliberalism that served as its intellectual scaffolding. We were right in the epicenter of the Asian financial crisis that broke out in 1997, and Focus quickly gained a reputation as a fierce critic of the International Monetary Fund (IMF) and an advocate of capital controls. We were part of the global civil society offensive that contributed to the collapse of the WTO's third ministerial in Seattle in 1999 and its fifth ministerial in Cancun in 2003.

Today, with the collapse of the WTO's Doha Round of trade negotiations and the crisis of legitimacy of the IMF and the World Bank, Focus is reorienting its work to place the priority on coming up with alternatives to the current system of multilateral global governance and to neoliberal approaches to trade and development. Our approach is called "deglobalization", to capture the necessity of dismantling the institutions of corporate-driven globalization in order to bring about a truly just international economy, participation in which leads to the strengthening, not the disintegration of those national economies that participate in it.

Focus has been part not only of the global justice movement, but also of the movement against empire and for genuine peace and security. We have not only produced studies proposing alternatives to the current imperial system to which war is endemic. We have also organized peace missions—to the island of Basilan in the Philippines, where US Special Forces were deployed in 2002 as part of the so-called War on Terror; to Iraq in March 2003, in a last ditch effort to prevent the US invasion; and to Lebanon in the summer of 2006, to witness Israel's horrific bombing of Lebanon. In March of 2007, we helped create an international network for the dismantling of foreign military bases.

I understand if people emphasize the strength of capitalism and US power in their analysis. However, while not underestimating the US and global capital, neither must we overestimate them. Globalization is in retreat, and the US is overextended, bloodied in a war that it cannot win in Iraq. The triple crisis of overproduction, overextension, and legitimacy opens up the space for alternative ways of organizing production, politics, and our relationship to the environment. This is a very exciting conjuncture.

So back to the question that we began with: why am I engaged? I guess I am engaged because I think one should do something worthwhile with one's life. There's nothing heroic about it. It's just that you have to do it, to be human. It's something we owe our fellow human beings, especially those who are marginalized and oppressed. We have a situation in the world in which this sort of exploitation and poverty that we have should have been banished long ago. Humans should be able to devise more equitable structures. And so one has to be part of that process. Because you either engage in the process and become true to yourself or you disengage from it and are just an onlooker. And that, I think, would signify not being true to oneself. So, the answer to the question why does one engage in the kind of work I do, is because that's the only decent thing to do. There's no great inspiration and no big heroism hidden in it. It's not a sort of martyrdom and nothing glorious—it's just pure decency. That's at least what motivates me.

Suggested Reading

Bello W (1982) *Development Debacle: The World Bank in the Philippines*. San Francisco: Food First.

Bello W (2002) *Deglobalization: Ideas for a New World Economy*. London: Zed.

Bello W (2005) *Dilemmas of Domination: The Unmaking of the American Empire*. New York: Henry Holt.

Bello W (2007) *Walden Bello Presents Ho Chi Minh*. London: Verso.
Bello W (2008) The World Social Forum at the crossroads, http://www.ipsterraviva.
   net/TV/wsf2008/CurrentExtraItem.aspx?new=23 Accessed 27 January 2008.
Bello W and Rosenfeld S (1990) *Dragons in Distress: Asia's Miracle Economies in
   Crisis*. San Francisco: The Institute for Food and Development Policy.

Chapter 13

Drugs, Data, Race and Reaction: A Field Report

Katherine Beckett

My foray into public scholarship began in 2003, when attorneys from Seattle's Racial Disparity Project asked me to conduct research on Seattle drug markets and drug arrests. Prior to this time, my research focused on the politics of crime, law and punishment, mostly at the national level. Although I wrote about controversial political and institutional dynamics, I remained at some remove from my subject matter, as well as from affected and concerned publics. My collaboration with the Racial Disparity Project, however, fundamentally altered my work—and my perspective on the academic mission.

Seattle's Racial Disparity Project is housed in *The Defender Association*, one of several non-profit agencies in King County, Washington that provide legal representation to indigent criminal defendants. It has also received funding from the Justice Department, the Open Society Institute, the Racial Justice Collaborative, the JEHT Foundation, and others to conduct research and advocacy on issues that disproportionately affect Seattle's communities of color. On the basis of discussions with organizations working in such communities, judges, and others, attorneys from the Racial Disparity Project identified the drug war as a key issue.

When I was approached in 2003, the Racial Disparity Project was looking for a researcher to identify the racial and ethnic composition of those arrested for delivering illegal drugs in Seattle and compare this information with the best available data regarding those who engage in this behavior. Although I had written about drug markets and drug policy from a national perspective, I had not had the opportunity (or inclination) to delve into the dynamics surrounding local drug markets or the policing thereof. I was intrigued by the prospect, despite its obvious challenges, and agreed to conduct the requested research on behalf of the Racial Disparity Project. I had absolutely no idea what I was getting into.

The Seattle Police Department does not generally make data regarding the racial and ethnic composition of those it arrests for drug law violations available to the public. Yet it was evident to many working in the courts that a substantial majority of those arrested for drug law violations are black. This pattern is especially striking in Seattle, home to a relatively small black population and a significant, and largely white, heroin problem. Moreover, many of those convicted of distributing even tiny amounts of illegal drugs faced the prospect of lengthy prison terms. Who does and does not get arrested for violating drug laws matters a good deal.

Nationwide, the war on drugs has been an important cause of the unprecedented expansion of the US criminal justice system and of growing racial disparities in prison admissions. Although the political frenzy around drugs has receded, the drug war lumbers on, and roughly 1.5 million Americans are arrested each year solely on drug charges. Nearly half of these arrests involve only marijuana. Over three-quarter of those serving prison sentences for drug law violations are black and/or Latino. Even those who are convicted of drug crimes but not incarcerated may experience significant "collateral consequences", as a result of their conviction, including the loss of employment and/or income, access to public housing, educational loans and other government support, occupational licenses, and custody of their children. Some of those convicted solely of drug charges endure an additional and often quite harsh penalty: deportation.

In the hopes of remedying racial disparity in the enforcement of drug laws, and of preventing their clients from falling victim to that pattern, attorneys at the Racial Disparity Project mounted a selective enforcement challenge on behalf of a consolidated group of 19 criminal defendants. All of the defendants were black and/or Latino, and all had been arrested for delivering drugs downtown. Many were addicts who sold small amounts of drugs to support their habit. As a group, the defendants were alleged to have delivered narcotics weighing the equivalent of six M&M's (plain, not peanut). Collectively they faced the prospect of well over 100 years in prison.

I have learned a great deal as a result of this foray into the world of litigation and local politics. I have come to appreciate, for example, how important access to data is for those seeking to assess institutional practices and hold institutions accountable for those practices—that is, for democratic governance. Obtaining such data is often no simple matter, as many institutions (both public and private) jealously guard information that would enable the assessment of their practices and policies. In Seattle, for example, it took three years for the Racial Disparity Project to secure access to Seattle Police Department arrest data. These data were needed simply to ascertain the racial and ethnic composition of those arrested for violating drug laws. Selective enforcement litigation, such as that undertaken by the Racial Disparity Project, is one of the few ways in which data regarding the execution of the drug war can be compelled from unwilling officials.

My encounters with politicians and the local media have also been instructive. In these discussions I have found that evidence regarding racial inequities are all too frequently heard, and responded to, as the claim that individual actors are motivated by conscious, purposeful, and willful racism. Other ways of conceptualizing the issue—as institutional racism, as the manifestation of implicit or unconscious bias, as a failure to remedy practices that are known to produce racially disparate outcomes, or simply as evidence of racial disparity for which there does not appear to be a race-neutral explanation—are routinely pushed aside in favor of the question: "So, are you saying that the cops are racist?"

Not surprisingly, this simplistic way of framing the issue predominates in legal settings—where it sometimes appears to be mobilized quite purposefully. For example, shortly after an interview in which I stated that I had no basis to believe that King County judges, prosecutors or defense attorneys were racist, a prosecutor claimed in a legal brief that my research on racial disparities in Seattle drug arrests was tantamount to the claim that "the entire judicial system is racist against Black people". Even more disturbing, this unsophisticated way of framing the issue also prevails in public discourse, even among open-minded and enlightened individuals. The challenge for those seeking to expose and remedy systemic and institutionally produced racial inequalities is to identify alternative ways of framing these issues that lead to more fruitful political and policy discussions.

I have also come to appreciate that, academic arguments about the fractured and even illusory nature of "the state" aside, many state institutions act with a surprising degree of coordination in an effort to deflect criticism of government practices. The intensity of this defensive reaction, and the tactics utilized therein, have at times astounded me. A recent experience is illustrative.

In May 2007, I was invited to share my findings at a community forum on the drug war. Other speakers included a King County council member, the former police chief of Seattle, and a recovered addict-turned re-entry advocate. The forum was attended by approximately 500 people and received some attention in the local press. It was also televised and played on the Seattle Channel. Within a week of speaking at this event, I received a subpoena unlike any other I have encountered. The subpoena ordered me to provide, within 10 days, 16 categories of documents, including: "Any and all statements of Professor Beckett—written, electronic and otherwise—regarding race in the justice system, the studies she has conducted, and her personal and professional opinions dating back to 1999"; "All income tax returns dating back to 1999"; " A list of all persons contacted by Professor Beckett or persons assisting her, that were used to form the basis of her opinions and conclusions, and any notes, statements, or summaries of such contacts with these persons"; and (my personal favorite) "Any and all statements—written, electronic and otherwise—of any individuals that helped with, corroborated with, or otherwise assisted Professor Beckett in her work regarding race and the police and justice system, dating back to 1999". It is difficult to understand this subpoena as anything other than harassment intended to deter me and other critics from speaking publicly about policy issues.

Events surrounding the publication of our research are also revealing. In 2004, I and several co-authors submitted a paper summarizing our research on Seattle's drug markets and drug arrests to a leading criminology journal. In the paper, we showed that the drug delivery arrest rate for blacks in Seattle is 26 times higher than for whites.[1] We also considered various explanations of this pattern, and concluded that there did not appear to be a race-neutral explanation for this enormous racial disparity.

I was aware that our findings were politically charged. Still, I didn't anticipate how difficult it would be to get the paper published—even after it had gone through the peer-review process. After accepting the paper for publication, the journal editor received an unsolicited, six page, single-spaced "comment" which raised questions about our methods, findings, and integrity. Its conclusion read:

> The authors clearly have strongly held beliefs about drug laws and their enforcement ... Dr. Beckett's article is an advocacy piece that argues strongly for one point of view with a specific outcome in mind. It does not appear that the authors were willing to consider other available and relevant information which would have supported alternative explanations for the racial disproportionality in drug arrests.

This kind of "combat-by-bias" appears to be all too common. In my experience, those who design and implement institutional practices that have racially disparate consequences are extremely reluctant to engage in a meaningful and substantive discussion of the issue, insisting instead on the "bias" of those who raise questions and concerns about the practices that produce those disparities. In many settings, such allegations effectively deflect attention from the substantive issues at stake.

Sadly, such allegations of "bias" may also deter academics from involving themselves in public issues and debate. Scholars working in fields in which a naïve positivism that conflates objectivity with a lack of public engagement prevails may be especially sensitive to such allegations. In my own case, I was also constrained by my inherited belief that advocacy and sound scholarship are incompatible. Certainly, there can be tension between the two, as the ready availability of "hired guns" and the controversy over industry-sponsored pharmaceutical research suggests.

Over time, however, I have become convinced that systematic and thorough research is a key component of effective advocacy. It is simply not in the Racial Disparity Project's interest for me to ignore key data, unexpected findings or alternative explanations.[2] Moreover, research on an issue such as racial disparities in drug law enforcement is subject to many ruthless and exhaustive cross-examinations. In the course of sharing my findings regarding Seattle's drug arrests and drug markets with prosecutors, officials, and members of the public, I have had to account for nearly every coding, measurement, and analytic decision I and my colleagues made. Any errors or omissions will be detected— and emphasized by those seeking to discredit both the message and the messenger.

Through these encounters, I have come to think of objectivity more as a process rather than a state of mind. Objectivity, I have come to believe, entails the systematic consideration and evaluation of multiple perspectives, explanations, and sources of evidence. It does not require a refusal to ask difficult and unpopular questions, to draw conclusions based on evidence, or to share those conclusions, and the processes through which they were reached, with the public. Making, and insisting upon, this distinction is, I believe, of crucial importance if academia is to have any relevance to the public.

In the end, I have come to believe that the juxtaposition of objectivity and public engagement is largely illusory. Although it is true that I have taken a stand, I work hard to ensure that my positions and conclusions are based on a systematic examination of all of the available data and consideration of alternative explanations of key findings. Doing so is not only good social science, I believe, but a key component of effective advocacy.

Moreover, the opportunity to work with the Racial Disparity Project has allowed me to more deeply appreciate the limitations of the ivory tower ideal. Academic freedom is essential to scholars' ability and willingness to ask any and all questions, and to draw conclusions without consideration of their political popularity. In this sense, academia provides an important institutional basis for public and political scholarship. And yet I have learned more about drug markets, drug policy, legal efforts to remedy racial inequalities, cause lawyering, addiction, social inequality, local politics, and the many complex processes by which race comes to matter, through my involvement with the Racial Disparity Project than I could ever have imagined sitting in the confines of my office. In the end, objectivity—if understood to include depth and breadth of understanding—may necessitate greater political engagement on the part of academics.

Endnotes

[1] In the year 2000, there were over 39 drug delivery arrests involving a black person for every 1000 black residents of Seattle, but 1.5 drug delivery arrests for every 1000 white residents of Seattle.

[2] Both I and attorneys at the Racial Disparity Project recognize the need to tailor the legal argument to the empirical evidence. For example, despite the fact that the initial group of defendants in the selective enforcement litigation included some non-black Latinos, I came to the conclusion, based on the available evidence, that non-black Latinos were *not* over-represented among drug arrestees in Seattle relative to the participation of that demographic group in Seattle's drug trade. I never felt any pressure to alter this conclusion, and the Racial Disparity Project has since limited its claim of unequal enforcement to black defendants.

Suggested Reading

Beckett K, Nyrop K and Pfingst L (2006) Race, drugs and policing: Understanding disparities in drug delivery arrests. *Criminology* 44(1):105–138. Presents the results of our study of the nature and causes of racial disparity in Seattle's drug delivery arrests.

Mauer M and Chesney-Lind M (eds) (2003) *Invisible Punishment: The Collateral Consequences of Mass Imprisonment*. New York: The New Press. Provides a useful overview of emerging research on the "collateral consequences" of mass incarceration.

Mauer M and King RS (2007) A 25-year quagmire: The "war on drugs" and its impact on American society. Washington DC: The Sentencing Project. A succinct overview of the costs and consequences of drug prohibition in the United States.

Pager D (2006) *Marked: Race, Crime and Finding Work in an Era of Mass Incarceration*. Chicago: University of Chicago Press. An empirical exploration of the effects of race and criminal conviction on employment.

Western B (2006) *Punishment and Inequality in America*. New York: Russell Sage Foundation. A comprehensive analysis of the ways in which mass incarceration both reflects and exacerbates social inequality.

Chapter 14

Confessions of a Desk-Bound Radical

Don Mitchell

On a field trip organized as part of a recent conference in Hong Kong, I found myself seated on the bus next to a graduate student who had read a fair amount of my work on homelessness in public space. Sharp as a tack, he had also spent a fair amount of time in the US, and was passionate about the plight of the homeless both there and in Hong Kong. Rooted in a deep religious conviction, he was particularly interested in the elderly homeless and the ways in which they get caught up in the great maw of redevelopment, gentrification, and the privatization of public space. What he wanted to know from me were two things: my experiences working with homeless people in shelters and soup kitchens; and the specific actions that he and his comrades should take, *now*, to make conditions for the homeless elderly better. I did not know how to respond. While I have spent a little time in shelters and kitchens, I do not, in fact, work *with* homeless people—either as a worker in a shelter or as an activist in anti-homelessness movements.

This is a fairly common experience for me. As my work has become known as both radical and political, students, colleagues, and lay people frequently turn to me in expectation and hope. They expect that not only am I an activist (in the sense of someone engaged in organizing on the ground and seeking transformation through direct action), but also that I can provide useful ideas about how to be a more effective activist. Even more, they look to me as someone who will have good ideas about how to meld activism and academic work. In response, I always feel poised to disappoint, especially since on a fieldtrip bus, or in the hurried correspondence of email, it always seems so impossible to justify why I am not, really, an on-the-ground activist. In fact I think there is a real need for what could be called "desk-bound radicals" in any struggle for social change, and I hope that in this short essay I can provide some justification for this stance.

The Activism–Academics Divide

Debate and worry over the relationship between activism and academics is perennial. In my email inbox right now, for example, is a note from a student outlining his concerns that progressives and radicals have "retreated" to the academy, pulled back from direct engagement with the problems of the world, sought refuge in intellectual debates and the shallow politics of "theory". There is much of substance in this concern. There is no doubt, for example, that the defeats across the globe of the activist and revolutionary Left in the period after 1968, and the repressions that were part of these, led many into the relatively safe precincts of the university. Michael Watts, following Rudi Dutschke and others, argues, however, that such a move should not be seen only as a "retreat", but also, and perhaps more accurately, as part of a "long march through the institutions" that has instigated wholesale social change, not only of the academic universe, but equally of so many aspects of everyday life (Watts 2001). These include the mainstreaming of women's rights, environmentalist discourse, multiculturalism in the schools and the workplace, etc. None of these advances are complete, none are uncontested, none are fully secured, but all are real.

Several years ago I gave a paper at a session organized by the Working Class Studies Caucus of the American Studies Association at its conference in Detroit. The organizers asked me to present a paper on class and landscape. To do so I studied the history of the Dodge Revolutionary Union Movement (DRUM) and its successor the League of Revolutionary Black Workers. Active in the 1960s, both organizations were instrumental in the transformation of the Detroit industrial and racial landscape. They had worked through direct action, through the ballot box, and through propaganda. There was a moment, in the late 1960s, when revolutionary change really seemed possible. Even if revolution never happened, the transformative effects of the movement were clear.

One of the organizers of the session invited General Baker, one of the founders of DRUM and the League, to hear my presentation. He was graceful in his correction of my historical errors, but what I remember most from meeting him was a conversation we had later. By the time I met him Baker had been a revolutionary activist for four decades. He had been jailed, blacklisted, and hounded by state and corporate police and provocateurs. When I met him he was working the graveyard shift at the River Rouge steel mill (part of Ford). He said he preferred working that shift so he could spend his days in education—in organizing Marxist study groups, primarily—and in community work. He said that, at the current moment, there was nothing more important than study, nothing more important than the hard work of thinking through tough concepts to come to a better understanding of the world, how it is shaped, and where there might be opportunities to intervene.

For Baker, Marxism provided precisely the analytical tools needed both to understand the current moment and to anticipate future opportunities. Indeed, he told me that the most important lesson he had learned as a revolutionary was that one had to pay attention to historical time and circumstance. Conditions in the 1960s were ripe for direct revolutionary action; now they are not. But that did not mean one should do nothing. Rather, the most important task now was to prepare the intellectual (and organizational) ground, so that revolutionaries were ready—ready to be active rather than reactive—when circumstances changed. Study, research, thinking, working out analyses: these were the crucial tasks of the historical moment, so that the next historical moment would not be missed. Refocusing revolutionary activity from action to academics, as it were, was a historical necessity. Activism and academic work—and Baker made it clear that he saw aspects of university research and teaching and his study groups as part of a continuum—were not, *or should not be*, divided, but different aspects of revolutionary praxis.

The People's Geography Project: An Intellectual as much as an Activist Endeavor

Activism takes many forms. One we rarely think about is the popularization of knowledge so that knowledge may be better oriented towards and aligned with popular struggles. In 1995, I wrote a review essay on the social history, "Who built America?" Reading these volumes, which tell the history of the United States from the bottom up, got me thinking about what a popular radical geography might look like. Could geographers, more than 25 years after the explosion of radicalism in the field, really answer the question, who built America?

A few years later, in the hopes of beginning to answer this question, I began the People's Geography Project (PGP). The idea of the PGP was to bring together radical and critical scholars to work collectively in the project of popularizing radical geographical knowledge. It was my conviction then, and it remains my conviction now, that the theoretical, political, and empirical work that radical and critical geographers have conducted over the past generation is important not only intellectually, but also practically. It is also the case that geographic ideas and theories are little known outside the discipline. There was, I thought, a great need to *translate* geographical knowledge into languages more immediately available to those not steeped in our own traditions, ways of thought, and intellectual discourses. So the PGP was founded, first, to address this need.

It was founded, in other words, as an explicitly *intellectual* project: a project for bringing *ideas* into popular consciousness. It was therefore also an *activist* project in the sense that it sought to orient geographical knowledge towards programs of radical social change, towards the struggle for social justice. In that regard, the PGP was also rooted in an argument David Harvey made long ago. He wrote:

> The geography we make must be a *peoples' geography*, not based on pious universalisms, ideals and good intents, but a more mundane

enterprise that reflects earthly interests, and claims, that confronts
ideologies and prejudice as they really are, that faithfully mirrors
the complex weave of competition, struggle, and cooperation within
the shifting social and physical landscapes of the twentieth [and
twenty-first] century. The world must be depicted, analyzed, and
understood not for what we would like it to be but as it really is,
the material manifestation of human hopes and fears mediated by
powerful and conflicting processes of social reproduction. Such a
peoples' geography must have a popular base, be threaded into the
fabric of daily life with deep taproots into the well-springs of popular
consciousness. But it must also open channels of communication,
undermine parochialist world views, and confront or subvert the power
of the dominant classes or the state. It must penetrate the barriers to
common understandings by identifying the material base to common
interests. Where such a material base does not exist, it must frankly
recognize and articulate the conflict of equal and competing rights
Harvey (2001:116–117).

The goal of the PGP was to begin a process of translation, to weave
new worlds of popular consciousness by bringing radical geographical
knowledge to the fore. To meet that goal, a dozen geographers met in New
York City in 1999 to map out the contours of the Project. We decided on
several goals: a book-length *People's Geography of the United States*;
a comic book of radical geography; a series of pamphlets examining
particular events or processes (eg the geography of the United Auto
Workers strike of 1998 or the geography of the global anti-war protests
of 2003). We also discussed the use of other media like film and the
web, and we organized sessions at national and international meetings.

Ultimately we have achieved few of these goals. The terrorist attacks
of September 11, 2001 reoriented our work. Those of us based at
Syracuse University (including a lot of students) responded to the
attacks by creating a clearing house of materials for progressive teachers
and professors seeking to understand and explain the attacks—and the
reactions they called up—in their historical–geographic and geopolitical
context. That project was as intensely time-consuming as it was urgent.
(We repeated this effort in the run-up to the war against Iraq.)

There were other reasons for failure as well. One of these was
intellectual. We never figured out, or I should say we have not yet figured
out, how to tell the story of the people's geography of the United States.
All the pieces are there, and we know where to find them. We know the
components—the processes and struggles, the relations of power, the
imperialist endeavors—that go into producing American geographies.
But we have not been successful in apprehending how to *limit* those
components so as to tell a compelling yet still relatively complete story.

The great advantage of social historians is that they can use the
inexorable unfolding of time as a scaffolding upon which to hang a

narrative. The great disadvantage of geographers is that we know that space does not simply unfold, but constantly collapses, and folds over on itself, and that it *internalizes* processes in all their complexity: that is its very production. This is an enormously difficult story to tell, except in fragments.

Another reason for the failure was structural. University work is time-consuming. The demands of our classes, our own research projects, and our administrative work, while all important, also limit the amount of time available for working out a complex project of popularization. It was hard for us to meet and it was hard to carve out time to devote to the *People's Geography of the United States* book. Unlike writers, we cannot work at our craft fulltime.

In the midst of this two important things happened. First, innumerable others—in the US, Japan, the UK, Hong Kong, Italy, Australia and elsewhere—picked up on the idea of a people's geography and took it in new directions, turning it into their own project. The very idea of a people's geography has had resonance and traveled effectively around the globe. Meanwhile, the notion of a people's geography has changed in the process (as two examples, see http://academic.evergreen.edu/ curricular/empire/ in Washington State and http://peoplesgeography. com/ in Australia).

Second, the hard work of thinking critically about reaching popular audiences has proven vital in the way I have rethought local political engagements. I helped shape the Syracuse Hunger Project, which is a project of social service providers, activists, and academics seeking to analyze the changing geographies of food insecurity in Central New York so as both to better address immediate needs and to find ways to rethink the structural roots of hunger in our city. Second, I aided in the creation of a "community geographer" position at Syracuse University. This person's job is to work with local organizations in similar analyses of other significant social, economic, and political processes and problems.

In both these cases a significant portion of the work is devoted to showing how and why critical geographical knowledge is now vital to a good understanding of those structures of injustice against which we fight. For me, personally, the work of the Hunger Project and the Community Geographer ties me even more tightly to my desk: it is my responsibility to shift departmental funds to support such work (and thus to do the necessary work of winning consent within the department); to schmooze administrators who provide funding and resources; to write grant proposal after grant proposal (and go to meeting after meeting with foundation directors) in order to the keep the projects going. As part of that process I have had to find ways to articulate, very quickly and briefly, just why critical (and even radical) geographical knowledge *matters*— that is to do verbally (and in the context of grant applications) exactly that which the People's Geography Project set out to do: to explain just how and why thinking geographically and radically makes a difference to how we understand the production of the worlds of which we are a part.

Both the Hunger Project and the Community Geographer are limited in their transformative goals and I have had to learn to negotiate a fine line between a set of reformist and sometimes even paternalistic projects and relationships on the one hand, and the radical politics to which I am committed on the other. In so doing it helps me to recall the lesson that General Baker sought to instill, the lesson of learning to assess the moment and prepare the ground. Remembering that moment helps me recall why my deskbound work, problematic as it sometimes can be, might also be critical in the current moment.

The Hunger Project *has* changed the geography of food security (helping to shift the locations and opening hours of emergency pantries, for example, to better meet the needs of the working poor); its analyses have proved vital in statewide advocacy; and it has led into more direct community organizing efforts (directed by neighborhood activists) by doing the analytical groundwork necessary, for example, to jump-start a community gardening program that has organizing as well as food growing as its central mission. The Community Geographer project, for its part, has led to the formation of a coalition of activists seeking to understand the structural effects of incarceration—and its racist geographies—on sending and receiving neighborhoods, a project that promises to be, in fact, a quite radical intervention into business as usual in our city. In both these ways, the Hunger Project and the Community Geographer in fact meet just those goals—of popularizing radical geography and reorienting it towards structural transformation— that the People's Geography Project established nearly a decade ago.

Conclusion

It is not hard to feel guilty when one's comrades are out on the line, marching against the war in Iraq, escorting doctors into clinics that provide abortions, or doing the hard work of organizing a movement in favor of the right to housing, when all you are doing is sitting at your desk trying to find the right words to describe the worlds these comrades are actively working to change. It is even easier to feel guilty when you are spending too many hours beseeching some foundation or another to give you a few thousand dollars to sustain such an obvious position as the Community Geographer. Such guilt makes it hard to remember, too, just why student activists in Hong Kong want to talk with me, want to seek advice and validation for their causes. They sought me out precisely because I do take the time to search for those telling words, to undertake the research that gives those words their force, to find those few thousand dollars, and to orient my explanations of the world towards exactly the change they hope to make. That intellectual work, and that bureaucratic work, it seems to me, are both vital parts of any activism even when, or especially because, it so often feels like the opposite of the kinds of direct engagement with the world, the throwing of lives on the line, that so many others so selflessly and effectively do. It is time to stop seeing the different roles we may play in social movements as a divide between activists and academics, and see it instead as an important and necessary division of labor.

Suggested Reading

American Social History Project (1989, 1992) *Who Built America*. Volumes 1 and 2. New York: Pantheon. A remarkable and accessible social history of the US that could be a model for similar work in geography.

Harvey D (2001 [1984]) On the history and present condition of geography: A historical-materialist manifesto. In *Spaces of Capital* (pp 108–120). New York: Routledge. Lays out an agenda for geography that is still relevant more than 20 years later; argues that geography must be historically grounded and oriented towards peoples' real needs.

Watts M (2001) The progress in human geography lecture: 1968 and all that. . . *Progress in Human Geography* 25:157–188. Traces the evolution of leftist thinking and activism after 1968 and the effects that the migration of much leftist politics into the academy has had on the nature of social movements.

Chapter 15

Becoming a Public Scholar to Improve the Health of the US Population

Stephen Bezruchka

The business community needs peace to see economic growth. They need kids to be educated to be consumers and workers[1]

As someone who has been teaching since 1967, I have always grappled with the purpose of an education. I began by teaching university level mathematics at Harvard University when I was a graduate student there. I went on to teach medical students and non-literates in a remote region of the Himalaya, as well as doctors, nurses, and various other health professionals both in the US and in Nepal. My scholarly efforts over the last decade and more have been related to new understandings I have gained about population health. These insights have led to the desire to improve the situation for future generations, whether they be my direct descendants or people in far-off lands. Describing how I came to this juncture may be relevant to readers interested in their own health and confused about the many health messages to which we are exposed.

After studying mathematics I went to Stanford Medical School because I wanted to do something obviously useful for society. In the year between my application and when I entered medical school, my character was transformed by time spent in Nepal, one of the poorest countries in the world. Instead of my previous career goal of applying mathematical modeling to cancer processes, I decided that I wanted to help ordinary people more immediately and more directly. In my first years as a medical student I became aware that while the US was the richest and most powerful country in the world, it was no longer among the healthiest, a position that it had enjoyed 30 or more years earlier. My teachers pointed out that while our overall health in this country improved, we did not improve as quickly as people in other rich countries. Since my professors did not seem concerned by this, neither was I. I trusted in them and the educational process to give me insight into what was important and what needed to be changed.

In the ensuing decades I practiced medicine in diverse environments, some lacking the benefits of twentieth-century technology, while others had the latest and best equipment available. Through practice, I learned that medical care was not what made populations healthy. I was unsure what did. At the time when I entered medical school there were about a dozen countries healthier than the United States. By 1990, 20 enjoyed better health. I could no longer contain my ignorance of why this was happening and went to public health school to find out. I hoped I would get answers at Johns Hopkins University, which had the biggest and reputedly the best public health school in the world. There I learned that since funders were not asking that question, no answers were forthcoming.

My professors affirmed that medical care had little to do with the health of populations; social, economic and political factors were far more important. By 1995 I was confident of research results demonstrating that the range of economic hierarchy in many societies, the gap between rich and poor, was causally associated with the health of that society. The mechanisms relate to the psychosocial theory of health in much the same way that the germ theory of disease led to the sanitation movements over a hundred years ago. In the ensuing years I have developed the skills to speak about these findings to various public groups, including the homeless, doctors, and academics. I have also written for publications that reach many audiences—from citizen groups, to the popular press, to homeless advocates and communities, to academic journals. My speeches have been broadcast on public radio and I have gained some access to television in my quest to inform ordinary people about the basic concepts of population health. During this period, our health as a nation, compared to other countries, has continued in its decline, and we are now about as healthy as Cuba, the nation we've been strangling economically for almost 50 years.

The ideas behind population health and its clear connection with political and economic factors are quite simple, but I have had only limited success in drawing public awareness to this concept. Our health as a nation is determined by the political decisions we make on how to care for and share with one another. People in the United States die much younger than they should, if the standard of health is a comparison between ourselves and other rich nations. No one who investigates the data can come to any other conclusion. Yet because of the overwhelming emphasis on consumption in our society, the knowledge and critical thinking skills required to make this assessment are lacking.

Personal health behaviors, the usual do's and don'ts that I preached for years, matter only a little. Furthermore, medical care does not do much either. The US spends the equivalent of half of the world's health care bill, yet more than 30 nations are healthier than ours in terms of the overall health and longevity of the population. I've had to confront these observations and unlearn much of what I was taught in medical school. It's not that what I learned was factually wrong, it was just not useful for producing healthy populations. I then had to relearn what matters. I have now chosen to teach what I learned. In this process I have had to look critically at the whole education process, and to realize that much of what we are taught is correctly described by the former UNICEF director, Carol Bellamy, whose quote begins this piece. We are taught to be consumers and workers.

The end of the Cold War could have resulted in rethinking our national budget priorities. However, by then we were already in the race to give the rich ever more and increase the gap between the rich and the rest of us to levels not seen since before the Great Depression. Because this is the direct cause of our poor health status, we are dying younger than we should, and are clueless of the reasons. It is the perfect crime. No one will ever be caught for causing this structural violence whose death tolls are far greater than the visible violence before our eyes every day.

What should we do about this perfect crime? The first steps are in creating awareness. We die much younger than we should, and the reason stems from adopting the neoliberal economic agenda that lets the rich take as much as they can in the expectation that some will trickle down to us. To challenge this prevailing wisdom and suggest it is not good for us is more difficult than landing on the moon. It requires a paradigm shift comparable to what Copernicus faced when pointing out that our planet was heliocentric. The Church did not accept this for over 200 years.

How do we come to hold such beliefs? How do we come to know things are true? I put this question to an eighth grade class recently. After the inevitable silence, one child responded, "if our parents tell us when we are very young, if our teachers and friends say the same things, and if we've experienced it". This epistemologist knows. My university students learn critical concepts of population health by teaching others and by appraising the academic literature. We have a Population Health Forum where we all struggle with how to inform about the determinants of health of populations and agitate for change. In order to not get discouraged we need a realistic time frame in which to expect progress. The resulting racism still present a century and a half after abolition provides a time line.

My academic work is directed at encouraging students and citizens to develop critical thinking skills, coupled with the types of awareness that they can use as lifelong scholars and activists in improving societal outcomes. Students can gain credit in the undergraduate and graduate courses I teach in population health by incorporating elements of public scholarship and activism. I suggest students assess their skills and do what they are good at, what they enjoy, and what they might continue doing for very long periods of time. Some students teach classes in middle and high school, others hold community meetings or speak in public places, some work with couples contemplating marriage, while others produce educational materials such as websites, posters, and graphics. They hold direct discussions in ante-natal clinic waiting rooms or in virtual meetings on bulletin boards and other internet avenues.

I tell my students that, if something is important to them, they should not accept a word of what I say uncritically, but rather look at the information and figure it out for themselves. This represents public scholarship, namely thinking critically for oneself and engaging others in your thoughts. I remark that we don't have a democracy in the US; instead, we hold an auction for our national leaders. They then have to confront what they think a democracy is, as well as the implications of the low voter turnout in the US and what it means. They have to tackle questions around campaign spending, and the fact that no president in recent years has been outspent by his opponent.

Gandhi said, "Be the change you wish to see". We can talk and teach, but as role models we teach by example. I struggle with trying new ways to engage others in considering these ideas. So my students see me at demonstrations and marches. They hear me give talks wherever I can. An occasional student asks to shadow me to get a sense of what I am about. In their course work when they do dissemination exercises I attend to offer support. I recognize that it takes a long time after students start to wrestle with these ideas before they begin to internalize them and consider serious action. I might get an invitation to speak at a medical school where an undergraduate who took my course a few years previously now attends. I use this opportunity to speak to as many other groups on campus, radio talk shows, and public meetings as I can. There is no way to predict social movements or paradigm shifts. To teach and practice activism also appears to be a health-producing activity, at least based on the research evidence. So it is a win–win situation, a healthy behavior for myself and for my students.

The path I've chosen has few of the usual rewards. By not focusing on traditional scholarship to work on research proposals that span a few years and produce as many minimal publishable units as possible, I do not gain prestigious academic rank. Many faculty in my own department are not very receptive to these concepts because there is little support for such work and few have been exposed to thinking about health as distinct from health care.

I am vulnerable by being out in the public arena as a gadfly with no academic security. People who hear my ideas in public where I am seen as a representative of a well-known university have complained to the institution's president that I have biases and am not objective. This has led to my being reprimanded because public institutions are very sensitive to public opinion; the former political center is now considered very far left so there are severe limits to public credulity. All scholarship has bias. I ask my students to take a value-critical approach and try to lay out the paradigm from which they work. But many people think that knowledge is objective and facts are just that. I've learned not to engage in endless emails with anonymous individuals who try to get me to incriminate myself thus giving them a virtual paper trail with which to attack me. I respond to everyone who communicates with me, but have learned to be wary of anonymous screeds. In such cases, I offer to meet with them to discuss the ideas. They almost never decide to pursue ideas further this way.

I have also learned not to associate myself in public with a specific hospital where I work if I talk about health or the limitations of health care in producing health outcomes, or the studies that demonstrate medical care is always one of the leading causes of death. When I wrote an op-ed on this topic in a local paper and listed my hospital affiliation I almost lost my job for not clearing this piece with the hospital publicity department! I've also found it of limited utility to speak to medical audiences about medical harm. Marshall McLuhan said: "Only the small secrets need to be protected. The big ones are kept secret by public incredulity". Professional medical audiences in this country have guarded interests in these big ones.

Anyone who communicates with the public on political issues must be prepared for nasty critical attacks that have little to do with the ideas presented. These can come via threatening letters, emails, phone calls, and especially today, the anonymous blogosphere.

One also has to be careful with words and phrases used in public discussions. In the United States I try to stay away from using any word ending in "-ism" and have reasoned answers when I am called a socialist. In other countries this is not a problem. Even the word "activist" has a nasty connotation here—forget radical or revolutionary. Once people hear these words, they tune out. As someone who came of age during the American War on Vietnam, when such words were acceptable, I have observed a transformation of the political climate in the United States. Universities today are wary of critical thinking that transcends intellectual disciplines and suggests that our current neoliberal political dogma is not the utopian ideal that media hypes it to be.

How did I end up thinking about these ideas? As a child I had two lofty goals: to cure cancer or harness fusion. In graduate school in the 1960s my beliefs that our government acted in our best interests were shattered. After medical school I questioned the benefits of medical care that were often more hype than help for societies. I got a wake-up call after the supposed harnessing of fusion in a beaker in 1989 to focus again on bigger goals by asking what made populations healthy.

There is little support in the United States for trying to make the country healthy by political means. The focus is on health care. Do you want health or health care? The United States has neither and deserves both. I work for health.

What is to be done? I can offer a few suggestions for individuals who wish to enter the domain of the public scholar.

1 Ask yourself at every step whether what you are doing or what you are about to do is getting you closer to your goal. In setting goals, ask whose game plan they fit. Consider whether they are consistent with the broader cycles of life on earth.
2 Prioritize your life: whatever you do, consider whether it is important or not, and urgent or not. Try to not do things that are urgent and important, and do them when they are important but not yet urgent. Avoid doing what is urgent but not important. And fill the "not urgent and not important category" with pleasure.
3 There are two kinds of people in the world: those who are ruled by technology and those who use technology for valuable purposes. Try to be the latter.
4 Confucius said, "Find a job you love and never work a day". Do what you love that benefits the world and the money will follow if your needs are limited. The most important financial aspect of life should be to live below your means.
5 Be prepared to think critically about what you think you know. Much of our understanding, beliefs and values have been crafted by political structures that do not serve our species or our planet's needs. Don't believe anyone if what they are saying is really important to you. You have to figure that out for yourself. This may require un-learning what you thought you knew, relearning, and then teaching others what you have learned.
6 In trying to get other people to think critically, recognize that mere recitation of so-called facts has little impact. People have to be exposed to ideas when young, have it reinforced over the ages and have experiences that relate to new understanding. So be as creative as you can in presenting facts and ideas. Recognize it will take repeated exposures from different perspectives and in different settings.
7 Recognize that we are social beings, that we have the largest neocortex of all primates, and we also have the largest group sizes. Anything important for the planet done by humans has always been done with others. Lilla Watson, an Australian Aboriginal woman said, "If you have come here to help me, you are wasting your time ... but if you have come because your liberation is bound up with mine, then let us work together".

Endnote

[1] Quote in the *New York Times*, 3 September 2000 from Carol Bellamy, former director of UNICEF.

Suggested Reading

Alinsky SD (1989) *Rules for Radicals: A Practical Primer for Realistic Radicals*. New York: Vintage Books. The classic work depicting experience derived from many campaigns to help poor people fighting power and privilege.

Baker D (2006) *The Conservative Nanny State: How the Wealthy Use the Government to Stay Rich and Get Richer*. Washington DC: Center for Economic and Policy Research. Available at http://www.conservativenannystate.org/cnswebbook.pdf. Recent information relevant to the United States on a process at work throughout civilization, namely that those with power commandeer most resources.

Chomsky N (2002) *Media Control: The Spectacular Achievements of Propaganda*. New York: Seven Stories Press. A brief summary of how propaganda must work in a democratic society where it is the most powerful force shaping beliefs and opinion.

Cutting H and Themba-Nixon M (2006) *Talking the Walk: A Communications Guide for Racial Justice*. Oakland: AK Press. A practical guide to using the media for progressive purposes.

Frank RH (2007) *Falling Behind: How Rising Inequality Harms the Middle Class*. Berkeley: University of California Press. Frank thinks outside the box and presents current ideas about how the increasing transfer from the rest of us to the rich is not good for anyone.

Illich I (1974) *Energy and Equity*. New York: Harper & Row, http://reactor-core.org/energy-and-equity.html Accessed 4 February 2008. A radical thinker presents the less is more perspective.

Incite! Women of Color Against Violence (ed) (2007) *The Revolution will not be Funded: Beyond the Non-Profit Industrial Complex*. Cambridge: South End Press. Some say we live in an Ngocracy, namely rule by non-government organizations or non-profits. This may contribute to the problem as these essays demonstrate.

Population Health Forum, http://depts..washington.edu/eqhlth Accessed February 2008 our Forum's resource where you can find articles, talks, presentations, course slides, action items, and notices of meetings.

Rosenthal S (2006) *Power and Powerlessness*. Victoria, Canada and Oxford, UK: Trafford, http://www.powerandpowerlessness.com/ Accessed 4 February 2008. A family doctor in Canada talks about the role of political ideologies in shaping the power struggle.

Schniedewind N and Davidson E (2006) *Open Minds to Equality : A Sourcebook of Learning Activities to Affirm Diversity and Promote Equity*. Milwaukee: Rethinking Schools. Beliefs are shaped when young minds are molded in schools. That is where we must start and this book presents many tools.

Trapese Collective (ed) (2007) *Do it Yourself: A Handbook for Changing our World*. London: Pluto Press. Practical advice on setting up a self-managed social center, producing fliers, and much more that reflects activities undertaken outside the United States.

Welton N and Wolf L (2001) *Global Uprising : Confronting the Tyrannies of the 21st Century: Stories from a New Generation of Activists*. Gabriola Island, BC: New Society Publishers. Presents recent activist examples to learn from.

Wilkinson R G (2005) *The Impact of Inequality: How to Make Sick Societies Healthier*. New York: New Press. The best single source on the critical determinants of health of populations.

Chapter 16
The Humanities and the Public Soul[1]

Julie Ellison

What is public scholarship in the humanities and the arts? There are many meanings to these four keywords—public, scholarship, humanities, arts. Public scholarship itself is a recent term for practices that, while venerable in some fields, are still new to the arts and humanities. What are these unfolding practices and knowledges? In the humanities and in many areas of the arts, collaborative work of any kind is rare, and there is a weak tradition of partnerships by faculty, graduate students, and undergraduates with community and public partners, either individuals or organizations. Consequently, there is plenty of room for ambiguity and debate about definitions. In order to establish a clear starting point for understanding public scholarship in the cultural domain, therefore, I will begin with a strict construction of the word "public", referring to work conducted in a deliberately democratic fashion by peers impelled by diverse interests and a common public purpose. I will focus on the importance of multiplicity and complexity in work in the arts and humanities that is jointly created as a public good by academic and community collaborators.

When I was growing up, my father published an article in the *Saturday Evening Post*, one of many he would write for the *Post* throughout the 1950s, entitled "They eat smoke for love". It was about the passion of volunteer fire fighters. Still, that phrase, "they eat smoke for love", captures something about my father's own passion for writing, pursued over a long career as a journalist, novelist, editor, professor, and self-published social prophet. The bitter irony of "eating smoke" hints at the long odds of making a living as a writer. But the phrase also applies to the question before us now, to the community-minded love for a different kind of smoke—the fluid paths of imagination and inquiry.

The word "soul", in the title that Harry Boyte suggested for this essay—"The humanities and the public soul"—floats before us, unresolved and undefined, probably undefinable. The evocative power of that phrase, "the public soul", goes straight to the heart of the quandaries of public scholarship in the arts and humanities. The phrase captures the profound desire for meaning and feeling—for soulfulness—that attracts many people to the arts and humanities in the first place. Such emotion runs smack up against the spirit of professional rigor and the norms of professional success. These clashes can be fruitful as long as one attitude does not drive out another. In order to craft the relationship between meaning and feeling in a public fashion, we must grapple with the mixed aspirations perpetually circulating within and between academic and community cultures.

Humanists and artists are always called upon to explain what the humanities are. What is art? Less interesting than the myriad definitions we summon up in response to these queries are the broader associations that cluster around such terms. To many, these disciplines broadly signify expression and inspiration—in sum, they are about *being moved*. They are also identified with analysis, theory, and critique. Artists and humanists in and out of the academy fret about how to negotiate the tension between hope and opposition, desire and critique, feeling and the labor of analyzing feeling. In public scholarship, these stresses become more pronounced. But at the same time, public scholarship can bring these tendencies into new and more fruitful balance. The defining feature of engaged cultural work is a determination to do it all, to undertake complicated projects that join diverse partners, combine the arts and humanities, link teaching with research, bring several generations together, yield new products and relationships, take seriously the past and the future. The driving philosophy is one of both–and, both mind and soul, both local and universal.

In this "both–and" spirit, William Paulson, in *Literary Culture in a World Transformed: A Future for the Humanities* calls for "an enlarged humanism" committed to "the project of enacting human freedom and working in the world in all its dimensions and directions". The agenda, Paulson argues, is capacious and transformative:

> an enlarged humanism ... locates our creative and constructive tasks as human beings not just in an aesthetic, intellectual, or even cultural sphere but in the entire project of making and remaking the social, cultural, and material collectives to which we belong (191).

History is helpful in establishing this vision of our future, including the history of hope-laden words. Nineteenth and early twentieth century intellectuals defined "genius", for example, in ways that we might want to take seriously again as part of our usable past. For them, genius— now so unfashionable—was an energy source that could fuel social hope, social labor, and social change.

In Anne Gere's study of turn-of-the-century women's literary clubs, she found that identity politics shaped the clubs' focus. Jewish women read Emma Lazarus, African–American women read Phyllis Wheatley, working women read Jane Addams. The clubs had a strong self-help orientation, striving to make women "more active agents" on behalf of themselves and their specific communities. At the same time, Gere writes, club members defined poetry "as the language of the soul and the inspiration of humankind", in other words, as universal. "Effective benevolence" linked to identity politics was central to the clubs, but these were understood to be fueled by the engine of efficacious greatness. Regardless of race, religion, or class, almost all women's literary clubs promoted the practical power of contagious eloquence by reading Shakespeare, Milton, Longfellow, and the Bible. The social place of eloquence—especially in poetry—is being reclaimed as the both–and logic of earlier eras returns in new forms. That logic held that poetry reflected the union of genius and history, that it served both progressive social reform and personal expressive needs, and that it was simultaneously universal, personal, and supportive of group identities. WEB Dubois framed black Americans' commitment to "developing the traits and talents of the Negro" as a program of "intellectual commerce" conducted by "co-worker[s] in the kingdom of culture". For Dubois, empowering the "Negro soul" in twentieth century US and international domains while also pursuing "time-glorified methods of delving for Truth", including those contained in the writings of canonical white writers, was a plausible agenda.

Academic humanists, now resistant to universals, suffer from the worst side effect of our powerful and necessary skepticism: we have made theory and action relative strangers to one another. The world of the humanities, as Paulson observes, suffers from "the overemphasis on critique, the mentality of a guild that fancies itself a counterculture ... and the excessive focus on reproducing the professoriate". Yet there is a strong and interesting tradition that joins the concepts of beauty, truth, freedom, and genius to the labors of social change and the advancement of the interests of particular communities. What if we recognized the ongoing life of this tradition and took it seriously? What if we respond to Paulson's revival of Kenneth Burke's "Literature as equipment for living" and begin to treat the arts and humanities "as a resource, as an extension of our collective sense organs, brains, and voiceboxes, near and far, then and now, which we can use as we participate in, and try to sustain, the life of the world". We do not need to reactivate nineteenth century notions of genius. But, like Paulson, we should commit ourselves to terms like "living" and "the world" that can carry a similar charge in our own day.

Speaking in hopeful terms, for those habituated to critique, puts us in a changed relationship to our cultural past and present. It confronts us with the history of words like "beauty", "genius", "inspiration", and, yes, "soul"—a vocabulary consistent with a desire for public speech and public practices.

Public scholarship in the arts and humanities most differs from standard academic practice through its explicit hopefulness. Such work is based on the conviction that it is possible for artists and humanists to make original, smart, and beautiful work that matters to particular communities and to higher education. Public scholarship provides a field for experiment, in which introspection and invention can be carried out sociably and publicly, yielding new relationships, new knowledge, and tangible public goods. The challenge for public scholars is to connect the difficulties of plausible hope with the emerging economies of cultural work. This connection can be made in leaderly ways. Models are available.

Over the last two decades, scholars have addressed profoundly civic issues: the history and meaning of "the public sphere" and "civil society", the importance of place, cultures of everyday life and ordinary people, the artistic and cultural achievements of women and racial and ethnic minorities; national and family memory, the life of the body, the power of stories to structure experience; the resurgence of poetry spoken aloud; and the layered histories of how artists and intellectuals are connected to their times and settings. Yet the public importance of the work of academic scholars in the cultural disciplines was declared to be vanishing even as their scholarly subject matter was becoming more inclusive and democratic.

What's happened to the humanities? is the title of a 1993 collection of essays about the academic humanities. The story it tells is a characteristic one of decline: "the humanities have become a more marginal part of [higher] education", afflicted by "declining academic status" and by "reductions in financial support" from the National Endowment for the Humanities, foundations, individual donors, and universities themselves. The contributors to this volume argue that the fading stature of the academic humanities leads to these disciplines being under-resourced. They protest that money is flowing to public programs and away from original scholarship. They lament the fact that, despite the fundamental human and public importance of cultural knowledge, the humanities increasingly are viewed as irrelevant. Scholars often deplore the fact that funding increasingly is tied to collaborative projects, with less support available for individual work in the studio or the archive. This pressure is felt as coercive, as sabotage of the conditions needed for imagination and reflection.

There are similar narratives of decline in the arts, pervaded by anxiety about cuts in funding for individual artists; selection mechanisms that keep radical or disturbing work out of contention; and the perceived competition between quality and accessibility. These pervasive worries about public pressures on the arts and humanities are not confined to higher education and are not unique to the US.

David Scobey summed up this state of affairs in his introduction to the Arts of Citizenship Program at the University of Michigan (http://www.diversityweb.org/Digest/Sm01/arts.html):

> The culture wars of the past decade have shown how deeply Americans are divided about their civic values—and how much they endow the arts and humanities with public significance. Academics . . . have pursued exciting new research into popular culture, the media, and civic values, yet our work has often been framed in ways that are inaccessible to the publics that we study. Partly because of this distance, the arts and humanities have been lightning rods for conflicts over such topics as the teaching of American history, ethnoracial diversity, and public funding for the arts.

Academics have plenty of legitimate concerns about the new public scholarship. For example, we have not begun to solve the problem of how to give public scholars time to think and write substantively about their work. How are we to combine our participation in communities of practice with writing? And the academic reward system is just starting to show signs of flexibility in the area of more responsive tenure policies.

The specific importance of public scholarship in the arts and humanities is to provide purposeful social learning, spaces where individuals and groups with "trustworthy knowledge" convene to pursue joint inquiry and invention that produces a concrete result. Central to this work is the crafting of "a politics of educated hope"—and "everyday politics" of coalition. There are real differences in the work styles, cultural agendas, professional status, and politics of artists and humanists working in diverse locations. But there are also productive points of intersection that mark potential agreement on what content is interesting, what aesthetic and thematic strands are most promising, what complexity is worth capturing. This, it seems to me, is the basis for "educated hope" about public scholarship.

One of the most important outcomes of public scholarship in the arts and humanities can be the integration of hope and critique. When I am collaborating with Chris Maxey-Reeves, a third grade teacher and my partner in the Poetry of Everyday Life Project, linking University of Michigan undergrads and Ann Arbor third graders, critique is fundamental. It is one component of an act of guided creation that we bring to the Ann Arbor Public Schools and the Ann Arbor District Library, to parents and kids, saying "We believe in this and so should you". We find ways to challenge university students and third graders to recognize and resist poetic cliché, for example, or to see through conventional idioms of beauty and emotion. On our field trip to a gritty urban park marked by the traces of the homeless people who live and sleep there, we work with the kids as they struggle to find words for their complex social knowledge of the half-seen homeless individuals who write fierce messages to park visitors in multi-colored chalk on the bridge. At the same time, we are not shy about proclaiming the power of agency, discovery, and feeling. We walk a fine line. You can celebrate something to the point of suppressing dissent, subtlety, and complication. But it is a fallacy to think that claiming the public good requires you to leave your intellectual tough-mindedness and creative ambition at the door.

What if campus-based artists and humanists—connoisseurs of metaphor—took ourselves more literally? What if we took the question of democratizing the canon literally enough to enter in the joint discovery of literary knowledge with non-academics? What if we took the passion for public spaces literally enough to collaborate with municipal partners on site design? What if we took our interest in gender and genre literally enough to work with high-school girls active in the poetry slam movement?

Finally, what if we learned what hope sounds like in public utterance? Here is an example of eloquence in the service of public scholarship, notable for its powerful complexity of vision. At the national conference of "Imagining America: Artists and Scholars in Public Life" in fall 2000, Dr Pearl Simpson spoke about the vibrant Black Bottom community that the University of Pennsylvania displaced and replaced in Philadelphia. She set forth how, in the enduring anguish of this site of so-called urban renewal, the Black Bottom Project created a full-length play based on the history of the neighborhood. The play was created and performed by former residents of the Black Bottom, University City High School students, and Penn students and faculty. For Dr Simpson, the value of the project was manifold.

"If you were, you were, and if you are, you are, and you deserve to be heard", said Dr Pearl, as she asked to be called. She continued: "We need ongoingness, we need refreshment, we need more people to take the place of those who go on to the great beyond because it's very important for everybody to know their history, regardless of how small or how minute the place. Some people want reparations, some people want recognition, and everybody wants respect".

The intricacy of Dr Pearl Simpson's statement mirrors the diverse project team; the neighborhood, school, and university cultures it traversed; and the pride and sorrow bound up in the fate of the Black Bottom neighborhood. Dr Pearl finds words for needs and desires ranging from economic justice ("reparations"), a place in the city's self-knowledge ("recognition"), a continuous link to past experience ("ongoingness"), hope for the future and solace for past losses ("refreshment"). She negotiates consensus and disagreement in the repetition of "We need ... We need" and in the sequence, "Some people ... some people ... everybody". The powerful moral and political claim to histories of a community's place, however "minute", establishes the premise for a multidimensional public scholarship project. There is no more compact or powerful witness to the ethical relationship between part and present communities than this: "If you were, you were, and if you are, you are".

What would a national laboratory for public cultural work look like? A fruitful ecology of public cultural enterprise is made up of local, national, and global networks of people and projects. At the local level, a modest economy of co-created work, grounded in broadly shared intuitions, carried out by campus and community partners, is subtly changing the zeitgeist in the arts and humanities. To bring this ecosystem vividly to life, I will survey the defining characteristics of a handful of exemplary programs. In so doing, I draw on the experience of Imagining America: Artists and Scholars in Public Life, founded in 1999 as a partner program of the White House Millennium Council and in 2001 as a consortium of colleges and universities.

What is Imagining America's agenda? Imagining America (IA) is a national consortium of individuals, institutions, and associations that puts cultural work in the public interest at the heart of higher education. IA is a network of artists and humanists who pursue integrative, multi-disciplinary project-based work across the town–gown boundary.

IA calls attention to a turning point in the dynamics of making and understanding culture. IA also offers an example for other disciplines to emulate as they reclaim their public soul and public muscle. It enlists project teams, program directors, and leaders in arts and humanities organizations, as well as university and college presidents. IA addresses the specific resources and challenges of the cultural disciplines, highly communicative and interactive fields with diverse practitioners and publics. IA offers information, convenings, models, access to leadership, and, most importantly, an evolving set of concepts and arguments aimed at constituting public scholarship in the arts and humanities as a movement. IA is both a learning community and a strategic advocate and citizens' lobby for public-minded artists and scholars and their many different partners.

Reflecting on the many extant examples of collaborative public scholarship in the arts and humanities, how do we move forward in the spirit of both–and practices? Michael Frisch, in his presidential address to the American Studies Association, delivered in Detroit in October 2000, helpfully articulates the non-reductive principle of both–and, which is fundamental to the new public scholarship in the arts and humanities: "the holding of different values at the same time without implying confusion, contradiction, or even paradox":

> In collecting . . . a book of narratives based on life-history interviews with Buffalo, New York steelworkers in the aftermath of the evaporation of a once-mighty steel industry, I was struck repeatedly by how regularly and easily interview subjects moved around the convenient categories presented to them—frequently of an either/or

nature ... They both liked their jobs and hated them. They identified with the union and/or the company yet felt betrayed by either or both. They saw themselves as victims of the plant closings yet refused to act or feel victimized. They were deeply nostalgic and yet fully engaged with moving on. They resisted the very notion that their lives were defined by their work situation, past or present, offering instead a more seamless web in which worlds of family, neighborhood, and community were woven together with work and workplace in their own identities.

Applying "different values at the same time" and different kinds of knowledge in public and community settings is an art that can be taught and learned. In a report on collaborations between the timber industry, communities, and government agencies, Steven Yaffee, Julia Wondolleck, and Steven Lippman of the University of Michigan's School of Natural Resources and Environment ask, "What facilitates bridging?" "Bridging", as they use the term, means collaboration among several different organizations. Their account of successful cultures of collaboration rings true for work in the public arts and humanities. They emphasize the presence of ambiguity, difficulty, complexity, and diversity—all characteristic of cultural work—in the situations that are best served by collaboration. The arts and humanities are sites of other key elements named by Yaffee and his co-authors: "a sense of place, an inclusive approach, a tolerance for small successes". All of these elements, they note, can be "intentionally promoted through creative efforts".

Collaboration, they argue, thrives in projects that the participants experience as fluid, uncertain, and calling for improvised strategies. In sum, Yaffee, Wondolleck, and Lippman transform complications that are typically viewed as barriers to community partnerships into conditions of possibility.

When conditions of discouragement become conditions of possibility, when ambiguity provokes meaning—making work, when uncertainty produces new knowledge, public scholarship in the arts and humanities has found its voice.

Endnote

[1] This essay is a revised version of "The humanities and the public soul", written in 2002 at the invitation of Harry Boyte, co-director of the Center for Democracy and Citizenship at the University of Minnesota, for publication on the Center's web site.

References

Burke K (1938) Literature as equipment for living. *Direction* 1:10–13.
Kernan A (ed) (1997) *What's Happened to the Humanities*. Princeton: Princeton University Press.

Paulson W (2001) *Literary Culture in a World Transformed: A Future for the Humanities*. New York: Ithaca: Cornell University Press.

Suggested Reading

Flores WV and Benmayor R (eds) (1998) *Latino Cultural Citizenship: Claiming Identity, Space, and Rights*. Boston: Beacon.
Gale S and Carton E (2005) Toward the practice of the humanities. *The Good Society* 14(3):38–44.
Hall DE (2007) *The Academic Community: A Manual for Change*. Columbus: Ohio State University Press.
Hayden D (1995) *Power of Place*. Cambridge, MA: MIT Press.

Chapter 17

This Fist Called My Heart: Public Pedagogy in the Belly of the Beast

Peter McLaren

For years, right-wing groups of all stripes have targeted me for my work with the late Paulo Freire, my writings on Che Guevara, my Marxist humanist analysis of capitalist society, and for the fact that I connect critical pedagogy with the struggle for socialism. My work in Caracas for La Cátedra Peter McLaren at the Bolivarian University, my educational projects with La Fundacíon McLaren in Tijuana, Mexico, and my affiliation with Centro Internacional Miranda, one of Venezuela's think tanks, has not endeared me to US neoconservatives.

Even so, I was surprised by the appearance of a ragtag group of scandal-mongering journalists pounding their yellow fists on my office door late in January of 2006. I had been preparing some speeches for the World Social Forum and the World Educational Forum in Caracas, Venezuela. Suddenly a pack of impatient hyenas were assembling outside my office, microphones in hand, spinning their corporate branded agendas for their big-network employers, demanding to know my reaction to being listed as number one on the Bruin Alumni Association's (BAA) "Dirty Thirty" list of UCLA's most dangerous professors. Treating me as if I had been placed on the FBI's most wanted list, they followed me as I fled out my office door and down the path to the faculty center. I wondered if I had entered a time warp and been catapulted into a scene from the Gilded Age of William Randolph Hearst's *New York Journal*.

I had been informed previously of some of the attacks by the BAA. They were unique in that they betrayed an infantile obsession with my physical appearance—my tattoos, my hair, glasses, and clothes. Because of this, I dismissed this group as simply laughable, although I was concerned that they had offered students $100 to secretly audiotape classes of leftwing professors and $50 for providing their lecture notes (we are not dealing here, after all, with mendicant friars). As frivolous as their maledicta and pro-Bush infotainment initially appears, these groups can't be taken too lightly. Despite the fact that their members are, for the most part, intellectually flatlined and disinclined to think critically, these groups have the uncanny ability to garner attention when they are able to lock interests with the corporate media, who always love a witch hunt. The malevolent attacks on me and my UCLA colleagues reflect an ideal expression of the dominant material relations grasped as ideas, and they continue to do their work of demonizing the left and making political dissent tantamount to supporting terrorism.

Scratch a theory hard enough and you'll discover a biography. In the mid 1970s, after a brief stint as a $50 a week copy boy at a national news service, I took a job as an elementary school teacher in a district that contains Canada's largest public housing complex. A child of the sixties (Timothy Leary wrote me a diploma that said "You Are Now Free" after an acid trip in San Francisco in 1968), I briefly studied to become a sculptor, and later switched to Elizabethan drama. I was filled with the revolutionary writings of Malcolm X, Eldridge Cleaver, Jean Paul Sartre, Frantz Fanon, Albert Memmi, Amilcar Cabral, Ernesto Che Guevara, Stokely Carmichael, the Beat Poets, and those of pretty much every leftist author whose books I could get my hands on. After five years of teaching what came to be known as "Canada's toughest kids", I entered graduate school, having published a controversial best-selling book on my teaching experiences.

While a graduate student I worked as an educational journalist, writing a regular column called "Inner-City Insight" for the teacher's union newspaper. My intellectual life became dominated by modernist writers and artists—liberation theologians, the Frankfurt School theorists, existential phenomenologists, surrealists, symbolic interactionists, Freudian and Jungian psychologists, Freirean educators, Zen Buddhists, performance theorists, ethnographers, ethnomethodologists, Gnostics, theosophists, Hegelians, historical materialists, comparative symbologists, Nietzsche, Lefebvre, Jean Genet, Charles Baudelaire, Franz Kafka, Leon Trotsky, José Carlos Mariátegui Karl Marx, Lenin (Vladimir Ilyich Ulyanov) and members of the Situationist International. Many of these disciplines, languages and thinkers taught me to face uncomfortable truths about the human condition, and to recognize and appreciate the power which can be unleashed in collective struggles to transform it.

After auditing a summer course taught by Michel Foucault (I had Foucault in the morning and Umberto Eco in the afternoon—in those days it couldn't get much better), and writing a doctoral thesis that was driven by the comparative symbology of Victor Turner, I took a job as a senior lecturer at Brock University's College of Education. Some conservative students, provoked by my radical politics, launched a petition to have my contract terminated at the end of the year. A larger group of students, who supported my classes, occupied the office of an administrator until the Dean agreed to renew my contract. The students graduated at the end of the academic year and, predictably, the Dean terminated my contract as if he were casually dabbing some Anusol ointment on an inflamed hemorrhoid.

After writing the Preface to the publication of my doctoral dissertation, radical educator Henry Giroux (who himself had been fired by Boston University's reactionary president, John Silber), set the conditions in motion for me to leave Canada and work with him at Miami University of Ohio. He considered himself in virtual exile there, but it was a place that gave him the latitude to create a Center for Education and Cultural Studies within the Graduate School of Education and Allied Professions. It was in Henry's company that I began to deepen my engagement with the field of critical pedagogy.

Critical pedagogy's once-subversive refusal to reproduce dominant ideologies and practices inherent in capitalist schooling and instead to embrace the possibility of resisting and transforming them has been tempered—domesticated, in fact—by the *soi-disant* politics of postmodernism. Postmodernists have become the fitting progeny of transnational capital. Rather than becoming preoccupied with the discursive ruptures, discontinuities, and arbitrary subjectivism of the postmodernists, I prefer to emphasize the continuity of capitalist relations of exploitation, maintaining that the struggle for social justice, and for socialism, can be grounded in non-arbitrary conditions. I believe academics must take a principled and non-negotiable stance against exploitation and oppression of all living creatures, one that strives for social justice and dignity for all human beings. And if this means inflicting a blow on history, then we are obliged to participate with all the force of Thor's Mjolnir.

I remain mindful of the Marxist humanist concern of revolutions turning into their opposite. And the question of what direction our struggle should take to make both of these concerns unnecessary (if not irrelevant) has been thrust to the forefront of my own critical pedagogy. It is a question that has been a preeminent one for me in my work both as a public scholar and activist.

Many of my academic colleagues, looking for some final vantage point from which to interpret social life, remain politically paralyzed, their studied inaction resulting from a stubborn belief that if they wait long enough, they surely will be able to apprise themselves of a major, messianic, supra-historical discourse that will resolve everything. Presumably this *ne plus ultra* discourse will arrive on the exhausted wings of the Angel of History! There seems to be some naïve belief that a contemporary codex will eventually be announced (no doubt by a panjandrum at an ivy league university) which will explain the quixotic mysteries and political arcana of everyday life. At this moment intellectuals will have the Rosetta Stone of contemporary politics in their possession, enabling them to know how to act decisively under any and all circumstances. Establishment academics under the thrall of technocratic rationality act as if the future might one day produce a model capitalist utopia in the form of an orrery of brass and oiled mahogany whose inset spheres and gear wheels, humming and whirring like some ancient clavichord melody, will reveal without a hint of dissimulation the concepts and practices necessary to keep the world of politics synchronized in an irenic harmony. All that would be necessary would be to keep the wheelworks in motion.

One thing is clear: the trajectory of history is non-linear. It is not mechanical. In the stretching and tearing, folding and collapsing of time there is only the now of our struggle, of the embattled toilers of the world. Daniel Bensaid (2002) writes that the key political task is to anticipate the present in the dialectical conception of historical time. The present is strategic, it is a suspended present, not a transition. It is a place where the past, present and future are non-temporal. It is a fork in the road. It is the crossroads. It is the time to struggle for a different life. A life outside of labor's value form. It is a time for teaching, a time for pedagogy, for the development of critical pedagogy—revolutionary critical pedagogy.

The struggle for a critical pedagogy is perhaps best animated by the poetry of Antonio Machado (1962): *Caminante no hay camino, se hace el camino al andar* [*Traveler, there is no road. The road is made as one walks*]. There is no predetermined path, but we can look to the past, the future and to the present to see possible directions that our struggle can take. We don't struggle in some absolute elsewhere, lamenting having missed our rendezvous with truth. Our struggle is warm-blooded and it will end where its gestation began: in the fertile soil of class struggle. We know where we are going, because it is the only destination where we can divest our human condition of its many disguises and even then, we need to realize that we can only contest the ideological production of the capitalist class and not abolish it unless the social relations of production generating it cease to exist.

The path to socialism, while continually created anew, is not a solitary one. Others before us have kicked up a lot of dust along the trail. Some of that dust is mixed with blood, and we need to tread carefully, yet not lose the determination in our step. And while workers may drop to the ground like spent cartridges in their conditioned effort to overthrow the regime of capital, their struggles exit the chambers of necessity with such an explosive force that history lurches out of its slumber in abstract, monumental time into the liminal present where the past is no longer and the future is not yet. Such a journey demands a critical pedagogy for the twenty-first century.

Critical pedagogy needs to be renewed. It can no longer remain as a bundle of classroom methodologies removed from a larger politics of socialist struggle nor a compendium of gnomic maxims that have a roborant effect on hardscrabble youth, such as "become an active agent of history rather than its casuality". It needs to be rhetorical, but not merely rhetorical. This time around it has to be concerned with the problem of reasserting human action, what we call praxis. The depredations of the postmodern pedagogues often subordinated praxis to the realm of ideas, theory, and the regime of the episteme. But critical pedagogy needs not only to disambiguate the otiose claims of the postmodernists and reject their cult of fashionable apostasy but begin with public political action, what has been called "public pedagogy".

Paulo Freire's (1994) work can certainly assist us in this endeavor. Freire has helped us to fathom the complex and variegated dimensions of our everyday life as educators. He has helped us, in other words, not to believe everything we think! As critical pedagogy's conscience-in-exile, Freire sought, through the pedagogical encounter, to foist off the tyranny of authoritarianism and oppression and bring about an all-embracing and diverse fellowship of global citizens profoundly endowed with a fully claimed humanity. Yet instead of heeding a Freirean call for a multi-vocal public and international dialogue on our culpability as the world's sole superpower, we US academics have permitted a fanatical cabal of politicians with impassible minds to convince us that dialogue is weakness, an obstacle to peace, and univocal assertion is a strength. We must reverse this trend.

All critical educational praxis is directive and political; it betrays a preference, a disposition. Freire argues that we find authoritarianism on both the right and the left of the political spectrum. It is true that both groups can be reactionary in an "identical way" if they "judge themselves the proprietors of knowledge, the former, of revolutionary knowledge, the latter, of conservative knowledge". Both forms of authoritarianism are elitist. Teaching should never, under any circumstances, be a form of imposition. When we teach critically we often fear that we might be manipulating our students in ways that escape our observations. But the alternative is not to teach, not to act, to remain pedagogically motionless. Teaching critically is always a leap across a dialectical divide that is necessary for any act of knowing to occur. Knowing is a type of dance, a movement, but a self-conscious one. Criticality is not a line stretching into eternity, but rather it is a circle. In other words, knowing can be the object of our knowing, it can be self-reflective, and it is something in which we can make an intervention. In which we *must* make an intervention.

We are universalists because we struggle for universal human rights, for economic justice worldwide, but we begin from somewhere, from concrete spaces and places where subjectivities are forged and commodified (and we hope de-commodified), and where critical agency is developed in particular and distinct ways. And when Freire speaks of struggling to build a utopia, he is speaking of a concrete as opposed to an abstract utopia, a utopia grounded in the present, always operating "from the tension between the *de*nunciation of a present becoming more and more intolerable, and the '*an*nunciation,' announcement, of a future to be created, built—politically, esthetically, and ethically—by us women and men". Utopias are always in motion, they are never pre-given, they never exist as blueprints which would only ensure the "mechanical repetition of the present" but rather they exist within the movement of history itself, as opportunity and not as determinism. They are never guaranteed.

Revolutionary critical pedagogy operates from an understanding that the basis of education is political and that spaces need to be created where students can imagine a different world outside of capitalism's law of value (ie social form of labor), where alternatives to capitalism and capitalist institutions can be discussed and debated, and where dialogue can occur about why so many revolutions in past history turned into their opposite.

We are constantly reminded of Che's storied admonition that you can't build a socialist society without at the same time creating a new human being. Echoing the question raised by Marx in his Theses to Feuerbach ("who will educate the educators"?), Che wrote in a speech in 1960:

> The first recipe for educating the people is to bring them into the revolution. Never assume that by educating the people they will learn, by education alone, with a despotic government on their backs, how to conquer their rights. Teach them, first and foremost, to conquer their rights and when they are represented in government they will effortlessly learn whatever is taught to them and much more.

Those of us who work in the field of education must subject the social relations of everyday life to a different social logic—transforming them in terms of criteria that are not already steeped in the logic of commodification. Students can—and should—become resolute and intransigent adversaries of the values that lie at the heart of commodity capitalism. This implies building a new social culture, control of work by the associated producers and also the very transformation of the nature of work itself.

We need to transform the social relations of production, including those extra-territorial economic powers that exceed the control of nation states. And we don't need a social state as much as a socialist one. We need to do more than to counter the damage wreaked by capitalism; we need to create a society outside of capital's value form.

This brings us back to the BAA. Organizations like the BAA want to bring about a New American Century in tandem with the goals of the Bush administration. They are fearful of the pedagogies employed in classrooms because they fear the power of critique and of dissent. Like a virus they would like to infiltrate those remaining social bodies, such as universities and public schools, where possibilities still exist for questioning dominant ideologies and practices. To make matters worse, many of these organizations have allied themselves with dispensationalist, premillenialist and pretribulationalist evangelicals.

To make my work more cogent and consistent with my struggle for social and economic justice, I've learned not to define what I do in the academy as being part of an academic career. I prefer to see myself as engaged in a political project, one that is inextricably concerned with co-creating protagonistic and participatory democracy with my students, pedagogical spaces where students can learn, and can learn from their learning.

Creating spaces for critical learning is difficult, since building reciprocal feelings of trust is paramount. Many students in university settings are reluctant to stay in classrooms where they feel they are going to be the objects of attack and derision. The goal of course is to challenge the experiences of students without taking away their voice. You don't want to affirm a racist or sexist or homophobic voice, but how is such a challenge accomplished without removing the student's voice entirely? I try to learn from my own experiences working with university groups that define themselves as progressive or radical. Recently I accepted an invitation to speak at a university on the East Coast, and my visit followed a public lecture and an exhausting seminar at another nearby campus. After my speech, I attended a dinner with several university administrators, one self-described Marxist geographer and half a dozen of his graduate students. As soon as the administrators left the room, the professor asked me in a tone if not pontifical, then at least parsonical, why I only "pretended to think" during my lecture. He and his graduate students (with the exception of one student with whom I had had a previous discussion) then began criticizing my talk as worthless, claiming they learned absolutely nothing from me and that attending my talk was a waste of their time. I was merely a fainéant rhetorician, an unavailing performer mired in the aesthetics of my delivery, collapsing critique into a chandelier of words, fit to be perched on Liberace's piano perhaps but not deserving of a lecture hall where an unvarnished Marxist riposte against the machinations of capital was expected.

Their glib and scabrous comments could have been as easily delivered by Daddy Warbucks as by the well-nigh flawless thinkers with whom I was sharing sacred space. I am used to being inordinately criticized, and relish a productive debate, but criticism as a politics of affective "play" is another matter. Not once was I asked to clarify my position on any issue, to unscroll the message hidden beneath what was presumed to be the sumptuously impenetrable artifice of my talk, nor was I asked to extend my analysis. The juvenile smirks of the professor and students made it evident to me that this was a form of sport—who can best target the visiting guest and strike home with the most debilitating remark, delivered in the most pestiferous manner. In this smackdown display of unenlightened false consciousness, there was no larger project involved pertaining to co-constructing knowledge as a group. There was no attempt to engage me beyond the realm of throwing insults. What concerns me is not a question of politeness. It is a question of pedagogical engagement and alliance building among those who profess to want to build a post-capitalist world. The experience reminded me very much of listening to the red-baiting hectoring of the Bruin Alumni Association. Clearly, more professors and graduates need to read Paulo Freire.

Public scholarship should be about achieving for humanity freedom from necessity. History, for the critical public scholar, can become a more steady vehicle for pedagogical initiatives able to frame present action in a critical fashion, incorporating as part of the process both the logic of the old and the logic of the new—as necessary expressions of the class struggle. Historical consciousness cannot be grasped through contemplation or critical self-reflexivity alone—activity confined to the zodiac of our imaginations. Even if wielded with vehemence against the capitalist class, these discourses of critique are insufficient for the kind of social and economic transformation necessary to defeat the turpitude of capital and its forces of exploitation. All of these pedagogical features— the employment of critique, consciousness-raising, and class struggle— conspire timelessly in the process of Karl Marx's "revolutionary praxis", as part of an effort to bring about a socialist alternative to capitalism. Revolutionary praxis, stressed Marx, is not some arche-strategy of political performance undertaken by academic mountebanks in the semiotics seminar room but instead is about "the coincidence of the changing of circumstances and of human activity or self-change" (Lebowitz 2007). It is through our own activities that we develop our capacities and capabilities. We change society by changing ourselves and we change ourselves in our struggle to change society. The act of knowing is always a knowing act. It troubles and disturbs the universe of objects and beings, it can't exist outside of them; it is interactive, dialogical. We learn about reality not by reflecting on it but by changing it. Paying attention to the simultaneous change in circumstances and self-change and creating a new integrated worldview founded upon a new social matrix is the hallmark of the public scholar and educator. Public scholarship is about understanding objective class relations in the context of historical processes and social practices that are independent of our volition or will. It is about how our subjectivities are created in relation to the production of surplus value produced by social labor. A public scholar is a critical pedagogue who creates opportunities for explaining the constitutive impossibility of capitalism producing equality because capitalism is structured around exploitation of human labor in which one's socioeconomic position is determined by one's position within the labour–capital social relation of production; equality under capitalism means the equal exploitation of human labor (Ebert and Zavarzadeh forthcoming). Many public scholars have been debarred from critique by the conditions of bourgeois property relations. It is difficult for them to comprehend how freedom is not simply a product of juggling discourses but of transforming social relations. The mutually determining relation between the active subject and the object of contemplation stipulates that we need to critique the social matrix out of which we have become determined since our human agency always bears the impress of material and historical reality. The public scholar is devoted to creating the conditions for critical consciousness, which in essence is political consciousness (which in turn is designed to illuminate the political unconscious that regulates the social totality) produced by ideological forces as well as the social relations of production and other attributes of the economic infrastructure historically in place.

The politics of participation with others (how we view and conduct ourselves as co-producers of knowledge) very much affects the ways in which we choose to construct our revolutionary praxis—including our pedagogical politics. Here we can invite students to recollect the past, to situate the present socially, politically and economically, and to challenge ascribed methods of producing knowledge vertically so that the future no longer becomes a reinitiation and recapitulation of the relations of power and privilege found in the present. In this way, professors can help students in producing knowledge reciprocally and dialogically, challenging the brute particularities of their subjective existence in relation to the larger socio-cultural and economic frameworks that give them meaning, thereby contesting the calcification and erasure of their cultural and subjective formations while at the same time dialectically and protagonistically refashioning their self and social formations in their struggle to become the subject rather than the object of history. History's osteoporetic spine can be crushed under the weight of the burden we place on it to find its own way. We can help it lurch in the direction of freedom only by apprising ourselves of the pedagogical dimension of the political and re-membering the political by living it pedagogically. And creating pedagogical spaces for self and social transformation, and for coming to understand that both are co-constitutive of building socialism for the twenty-first century—a revolutionary praxis for the present in the process of creating a permanent revolution for our times.

References

Bensaid D (2002) *Marx for Our Times: Adventures and Misadventures of a Critique.* Translated by Gregory Elliot. London: Verso.

Ebert T and Zavarzadeh M (forthcoming) *Class in Culture.* London: Paradigm Press.

Freire P (1994) *Pedagogy of Hope: Reliving Pedagogy of the Oppressed.* New York: Continuum.

Lebowitz M (2006) *Build It Now: Socialism for the Twenty-First Century.* New York: Monthly Review.

Lebowitz M (2007) Human development and practice. *MRZine* 9 April, http://www. monthlyreview.org/mrzine/lebowitz090407.html Accessed 27 January 2008.

Löwy M (1997) Che's revolutionary humanism: Ideals of Ernesto "Che" Guevara. *Monthly Review* 49(5), http://www.findarticles.com/p/articles/mi_m1132/is n5_v49/ai_20039201 Accessed 1 June 2007.

Machado A (1962) *Manuel y Antonio Machado: Obras Completas*. Madrid: Editorial Plenitud.

McLaren P (2007) The future of the past: Reflections on the present state of empire and pedagogy. In P McLaren and J Kincheloe (eds) *Critical Pedagogy: Where Are We Now?* (pp 289–314). New York: Peter Lang.

Suggested Reading

The following two books are by the great Brazilian educational thinker who is considered to be the most important representative of what has come to be known as liberatory education or critical pedagogy. These books do a remarkable job of linking the pedagogical to the political and the political to the pedagogical.

Freire P ([1970] 1998) *Pedagogy of the Oppressed*. Translated by Myra Bergman Ramos. New York: Continuum.

Freire P (1994) *Pedagogy of Hope: Reliving Pedagogy of the Oppressed*. New York: Continuum.

The following are two powerful texts by a scholar and revolutionary from Martinique who is considered one of the world's most preeminent thinkers on the politics and psychopathology of colonization and colonial violence and resistance. Like few other books, these outstanding works take us to the heart of colonial darkness and offer some urgent insights about what needs to be accomplished in our quest for decolonizing education and society.

Fanon F (1967) *Black Skin, White Masks*. Translated by Charles Lam Markmann. New York: Grove Press.

Fanon F (1963) *The Wretched of the Earth*. Translated by Constance Farrington. New York: Grove Press.

Chapter 18

The Surprising Sense of Hope

Jenny Pickerill

In 2004 I started a research project called "Autonomous Geographies", which was concerned with exploring the everyday lives of anti-capitalist activists. The project was partially inspired by my own experiences both as an academic and an activist. Along with another UK geographer, Paul Chatterton, I was interested in activists' experiences of being between disparate worlds: those incorporating the activist arena, and "the rest" (family, workplace, academia etc). How do activists accommodate these types of disjunctures and even use them creatively to make new spaces for anti-capitalist ideas and practices?

Unlike my earlier research, however, I was now in a permanent faculty position with a steady salary. Accepting that post just a year before appeared to be the decisive point at which I became a capital "A" Academic. At this time I began to struggle internally with whether my job precluded my being the type of activist (and person) I had previously perceived myself to be. Others were also highly critical of my new role. The following is an email from Jake (a pseudonym) in response to my invitation to take part in an advisory panel for the Autonomous Geographies project (February 2006, emphasis added):

> No matter how I look at this project—it just smacks of academics on-the-rise from so-called activist backgrounds who are finding a niche for themselves in academic circles with "activist" kudos. You flaunt a large sum of money, but promise very little "social change" potential from your proposed uses of this money ... *Political transformation [is] a by-product of your careers, not the other way around*. Getting involved in a project like Autonomous Geographies looks like it's uncomfortably straddling the two worlds ... Simply working within an institution frames your work. The political line will have to go somewhere down the middle because of this ... it is actually totally disgusting for me to see [you] ... becoming an "expert on the subject" in the eyes of the academy, and taking a salary for it, yet operating in a parasitical relationship to those who are doing the real work and have made financial/lifestyle sacrifices.

This resonated with heightened criticism from friends with whom I had previously taken non-violent direct action. They felt that I had "sold out" and was using my activist links to further my career rather than push for progressive social change. My negotiation of this apparent disjuncture between activism and academia is, of course, a personal journey, but it also reflects the ongoing calls within geography and the wider academy for academics to be more "active". This chapter is a reflection upon that journey and upon what it really means to be *active*.

Deeds Not Words

It was during the course of my PhD research that I became radicalised. Visiting protest camps to explore environmental activists' use of the internet changed and inspired me. I saw in those I interviewed a passion, commitment and quest for change that was lacking in academia and formal politics. The use of non-violent direct action, not just as a tactic but as a way of life, made change seem possible, immediate, and empowering. Slogans such as, "If not you then who?" and "Do-it-Yourself", awakened in me a new sense of urgency and desire for action. At the same time the work of feminist geographers encouraged me to see the power relations inherent in research, and the political potential of more participatory approaches in the design, methodology and production of knowledge. I began to understand that it was not just what topics we explored as academics that were important, but *how* we approached such topics.

This participation gradually consumed my life. I loved the thrill of being subversive, the amazing solidarity of friendships made in protest, and the empowerment of feeling part of something changing. Police confrontations and the incarceration of friends only served to deepen my commitment for environmental and social justice. But as the post-PhD prospect of becoming a "full time" activist drew closer something did not feel right. The more I worked on my thesis, the more I wanted to write. Although it was empowering to campaign, I began to realise my skills were not being best used. I was, frankly, not very creative when it came to ideas for direct action. It seemed that there were other ways I could use my love of writing, research, teaching and photography to good effect. This is beginning to sound like an apology or justification, the old adage of "those who can't, teach". It is not meant this way. Ultimately my political beliefs had not changed, but the outlet for my passions had. In December 2000, I left my friends defending a squat and our free food café "Mushy Peace", to take up a post-doctoral position in Australia.

This move was a deliberate attempt at a clean break. I wanted to reinvent myself as an academic-activist. In effect I simply tried to do both simultaneously without any real thought as to what I was trying to achieve. The result was sporadic, partial, and doubtless ineffectual. I overcommitted to too many campaigns, started too many projects and finished very few. Starting as a new lecturer compounded the irreconcilable dualism between activism and academia. Academia appeared to have taken over my life and I resented it. With a high teaching load, long hours and the pressure to publish in top journals, my activism diminished. Despite enjoying my new job I felt frustrated, a failure and a sell-out. I wanted academia to be more "active" and drafted several articles arguing such, but the hypocrisy of making "calls for action" while I did little, prevented me from publishing any of them.

"Good Work"

It is only in recent years that I have realised how blinkered I was. The notion of what constituted "activism" had become fixed, bound up in radical environmental rhetoric that direct action was not just the best tactic but a life choice. As a result, anything less felt ineffectual. I had disempowered myself of any potential to use the academy to push for social change, undervalued my own skills and failed to acknowledge the intricacies of political action, including the critical roles of writing and teaching. This ideological dead-end has been compounded by the plethora of academic articles debating how to make geography relevant, public, activist, moral and far-reaching. The authors of such polemics speak from concern at what constitutes "critical" geography and of the fear of becoming disengaged from their political passions. While they argue for different agendas they have one thing in common—they implore academics to "do more": more writing, more outreach, more activism, more empirical research. This, of course, is just my reading of such works, but as an early career academic the path to becoming a public scholar seemed to involve being superhuman. Being more "active" (in whatever form) remains an addition to, rather than an alteration of, all the other demands of academia. I would argue that we actually all need to do *less*, but do what we do better.

Our work for social justice should include our teaching and our everyday practices. I do not regard myself as anything close to being a "Public Scholar", which is far too grand a term for my small contribution. However, I am attempting to do "good work" in a way that appears to clash with a more conventional view of my role as an academic, but from which I reap rich emotional rewards. Recently I have steered my choice of research topics towards those where there is a real social need (increasingly identified by the groups with whom I work). Moving beyond my obsession with "deeds not words", I am now more determined than ever to fight the anti-intellectualism of parts of society and direct action activism.

The Importance of Methodology

Removing the notion that I am as much an activist as an academic from my research encounters enables me to practise a more ethical methodology. As many have noted, problems of objectification do not disappear simply because we share experiences through participation. The cover of "trust me, I'm an activist too" has been used by some to suggest that we can unproblematically straddle multiple worlds simply by dint of our political commitments. This belies our position of privilege and neglects consideration of power relations, reflectivity, and feedback loops. It also does little to temper the critique that academics are "taking a salary for it, yet operating in a parasitical relationship to those who are doing the 'real work'". Further, it can lead to the belief that participation is research in and of itself, obviating the need to undertake any further rigorous or in-depth analysis of others' experiences. This kind of participation quickly becomes self-referential.

I still undertake what might be termed "action research", and this has implications for my academic practice. In-depth empirical research is time consuming, slow and can be difficult to co-ordinate. It takes time to take on advocacy roles, be accountable to those one is working with, and deliver the different range of "outputs" that are demanded by all involved. Such a methodology has been core to my attempts to do "good work". However, I have been advised (by my academic mentors) to reduce my empirical work and spend more time writing theoretical essays. This approach appears to prioritise abstract over lived experiences and career advancement over good work. It fails to consider the risks of becoming divorced from the subjects of our research. Most worryingly it begins to remove the possibility of doing any "action research" at all.

Writing and Teaching for Most People

We also need to be critical of our roles as gatekeepers. There has been much discussion of the need to publish our work in more accessible language. Yet I would be a hypocrite if I were to suggest that we should all diversify our outputs; I'm well aware that it's only because I published in academic journals in an academic style that I gained a permanent academic position. Until we challenge our collective obsession with publishing in obscure, albeit highly regarded academic journals, graduate students and early-career academics will have little choice but to do the same. However, for those of us in a position of relative comfort (and this is much earlier than many seem to think) we have a responsibility to reprioritise how we write. It is not for others to decipher our work. We could so easily write more in the style through which we teach. This is not simplifying our analysis or undermining our academic seriousness, just enabling more people to understand it. As for format, there seem few good reasons why more of us cannot spend our time writing books and pamphlets, making as much of our material as possible freely available online (or available under creative commons licences), and livening up our work with better use of images.

Moreover, when we consider "outputs" from our work we often neglect the importance of teaching. I view it as one of my most important roles as an academic. Through teaching we can challenge and critically engage with our students and in so doing encourage them to critically engage with the world around them. I have tried to re-orientate my teaching towards task-based learning, and where possible introduce local day trips, based on the belief that by *doing* and *seeing* broader lessons will be learnt than from simply reading a text.

Instilling a belief that students can make changes and that these will make a difference (however small) is core to my teaching. It is not apathy that holds students back, but an inability to articulate and direct their passion while supporting their ideas with sound knowledge. My final-year students now have to put in place an action plan to reduce their carbon footprint, intervene in campus environmental management, and design material (including a magazine) that will communicate to a policy-orientated audience their thoughts on eco-house building practices. These tasks extend their communication skills while still requiring detailed geographical knowledge. Most importantly, I hope they begin to value their own agency for change and ultimately put such agency into practice. Moreover, I have begun to take my teaching out beyond the university and have readily accepted invitations by campaign groups to run workshops on my research topics.

Walking Your Talk and Creating Space for Passion and Hope

Doreen Massey has suggested that we need to bring "our lived practice more into line with our theorising *about* that practice" (Massey 2000:133). On one level that is a relatively simple and enjoyable thing to do. Treating others with respect, demanding equality, and living ethically is not hard if we are reasonably pragmatic about our attempts. I am not suggesting that there is not an urgent need for major social change, rather we need to think more carefully about our roles as people in that change. It is about our priorities and the value we place on good work; this "good work" must be valued above the other trappings of academia, such as career progression and recognition. It is also about focus, perseverance and balance. If I am to "be the change I want to see" and to live now as I wish to in the future then my lived practice must match my theories. This involves not just writing more clearly and in more accessible locations, but spending more time with my community, friends and family. It is about acknowledging that change starts at home. It is about creating space for passion in all of our life endeavours.

I used to believe that work was my passion but I now realise that academia has simply enabled me to follow my passions. This is an important difference. I only want to be an academic if I get to do good, political work. This may mean that I am forever destined to be caught in between competing demands, or relegated to the margins of the discipline, or both. There is messiness in bringing passion to an academic job.

I have been challenged, screamed at, and physically and emotionally drained by my research and teaching. I have made mistakes and been out of my depth. Yet I have also been inspired, warmed by the welcomes I have received, and motivated by those I encountered to carry on. Most of all, I have had fun. In the darker times, especially when dealing with those in stark need or who have suffered tremendous loss—such as Indigenous activists in Australia—there has been a surprising sense of hope. The horrors I have listened to have saddened and depressed me to my core. Yet with every story there has been a note of optimism. Always the hope of a way forward, even if we are unsure of the direction the journey will take us in. I want always to be listening, learning, and sharing that hope. For we can all have hope, and we can all use that hope to move forward together.

Suggested Reading

Massey D (2000) Practising political relevance. *Transactions of the Institute of British Geographers* 25:131–133. This short piece explores how we as geographers could make a more explicit political intervention with our work.

Solnit R (2005) *Hope in the Dark: The Untold Story of People Power*. Edinburgh: Canongate. This book documents the hope and optimism of activism, and the often hidden consequences of taking action to trigger social change. Using a broad variety of examples, Solnit argues that grassroots activists actually have great power and seeks to celebrate their many accomplishments.

Nearing S (2000) *The Making of a Radical: A Political Autobiography*. Devon: Green Books. Nearing reflects on his life as a radical. He became a noted freelance lecturer and writer in the US after being fired from academia for being too radical, and went on to practise autonomous living in Vermont.

Singer P (2002) *Writings on an Ethical Life*. London: Fourth Estate. A selection of writings on ethics and how to put them into practice. Includes reflection by Singer on his own journey through academia.

Chapter 19

The Making of a Public Intellectual

Howard Zinn

I suppose I became an "intellectual" when the reading of books, and playing with ideas, became dominant in my life, which was probably at the age of 17 or so. No one would have considered me an intellectual because I was a working-class kid who at 18 would become a shipyard worker instead of going to college. But, in the shipyard, I found young fellows of like mind and in the process of organizing a union of the young workers in the shipyard (excluded from the craft unions of the old AF of L) we met once a week to read and discuss radical ideas, from *The Communist Manifesto* to Jack London's *The Iron Heel*.

That experience made me aware that "intellectuals" are to be found everywhere, and not just on college campuses. This perception was reinforced years later when I worked in a warehouse, loading trucks with fellows who either were college dropouts or high-school dropouts (or in one case an immigrant from the Caribbean who had been a school teacher back home and now lifted heavy cartons onto the back of tractor-trailers). Among this odd crew were guys who read books and/or magazines, newspapers and talked about literature, politics and religion as we were hauling cartons that weighed from 20 to 80 pounds.

I continued to be an "intellectual" in whatever situation I was in, whether I was dropping bombs on European cities for the US Air Force in World War II, or knocking around at various post-war jobs, and then going to college and graduate school under the GI Bill and then beginning to teach.

Yes, but when did I become a "public" intellectual? That was when I took my speaking and writing, heretofore confined to workplaces, military bases, and classrooms, out into the world at large. It happened during my first teaching job, at Spelman College, a college for African–American women (called at the time a "Negro" college) in Atlanta, Georgia. "The Movement" was beginning to excite the South, after a long period of quiet, sub-surface actions and repressed anger in the black population, and I became involved, along with my students.

I would suppose that my first act as a "public intellectual" was to write an article for *Harper's*. No, it was not commissioned by them, for I had not published anything except my doctoral dissertation, which did not reach much of a "public". I had an idea, in 1959, the year before the sit-ins, that the South was ready for change, based on my observation of small, scattered incidents.

I had concluded that, despite all the dire predictions that white Southerners would fight to the end for segregation, there were things they valued more, that there was with them, as with all of us, a hierarchy of values, in which some values trumped others. For instance, bus drivers, who had threatened to quit their jobs if the courts ordered them to allow black people to sit in the front of the bus, when confronted with the reality, would value their jobs over their ideology.

When *Harper's* published my article, I realized that here was a way I could be useful to "The Movement"—I was in a special position, embedded (not artificially, like the reporters in the Iraq War) but naturally in the deep South, living in a black community, involved with my students, in sit-ins, demonstrations, picket lines. I could write about these experiences, drawing upon what I knew of American history and constitutional law (two of my classroom subjects) and blend my scholarship and my activism to produce writing that would be helpful in the struggle for racial equality.

That began my life as a "public intellectual", parallel with, but superseding, my life as a conventional intellectual, in which I was confined to the classroom, the seminar, the scholarly world. I was invited to join the Executive Board of the group of young people, veterans of the sit-in movement, who had formed the Student Nonviolent Coordinating Committee, and so could give what was presumed to be sage advice, coming from my research in history, politics, and law.

I began to move out from the college campus to places in the South where The Movement was in action. First, Albany, Georgia in the winter of 1961 and the summer of 1962, where mass arrests of black people protesting segregation had taken place, and where I was asked to go by a research organization in Atlanta to write a report. My report, which castigated the administration of John F Kennedy and the FBI for failing to protect the constitutional rights of black people in Albany, made the front page of the *New York Times*—that was as "public" as this intellectual had gone up to this time.

I was moving through the South with SNCC, into hotbeds of conflict—Selma, Alabama, and various towns in Mississippi—Greenwood, Greenville, Hattiesburg, and writing articles for *The Nation, The New Republic*, and other periodicals. When I left the South and in 1964 published two books on the South, *The Southern Mystique*, and *SNCC: The New Abolitionists*, I was not writing for my academic colleagues, but for the general public—yes, as a public intellectual.

This was not seen by everyone as a good thing. There were colleagues in Atlanta, and certainly college administrators, who thought it unseemly for me to leave the classroom and join my students in demonstrations in the city. And when these same students began to rebel against the college administration for restricting their freedoms, and I supported them, I was fired from Spelman College.

Moving north, I was hired by the Political Science Department of Boston University in spite of the fact that I had been a troublingly public intellectual in the South. My doctoral dissertation had won a prize from the American Historical Association, my book *The Southern Mystique*, while intended for the general public, had certain scholarly qualities and was published by a prestigious house (Alfred Knopf) and so my credentials as an "intellectual" seemed sound. My public activity had taken place in the South far away, and was all about racial equality, a movement which gained a certain respectability by now. And so there was not much threatening about me.

I was hired by Boston University in the spring of 1964, and that summer the fake incident in the Gulf of Tonkin became the excuse for a full-scale military involvement in Vietnam. As the fall semester began, I became involved in the anti-war movement. This public activity was not pleasing to the chair of my department or to the university administration. Increasingly they became troubled by my anti-war activity, my public speeches, my participation in demonstrations.

For the next two years, the tenure I had been promised when I was hired was not granted, with various bureaucratic explanations offered. But in 1967, despite disagreement within the department, my tenure was approved. Although I had become increasingly involved in the movement against the war, I had four published books to my credit and was receiving high ratings from my students, and that seemed to trump the negatives. It's fair to say I was now a full-fledged "public intellectual", moving back and forth from the classroom seminar to the street demonstration.

There was one kind of activity which seems to me one of the best ways to blend my scholarship as an intellectual with my work as an activist, and it was not something initiated by me, as were my writings, my Movement involvement. This was my increasing appearance in court to testify in trials of people who had been arrested in anti-war actions.

The war in Vietnam provoked many acts of civil disobedience— violating laws of trespassing, destroying government property, breaking and entering into offices—moving protest from words to action, to raise the level of indignation against the war.

I was called on again and again, as an "expert witness", with a background in history and political theory, to testify to the value of civil disobedience in bringing about social change. I was to draw upon my knowledge of American history to explain how acts of civil disobedience had been crucial at certain times to achieve a useful social goal.

As I explained to the court, it was an honorable and honored tradition, from the Boston Tea Party, to the anti-slavery movement, to the struggles of labor, to the actions of our own time. I cited the Declaration of

Independence as a seminal document of disobedience to government, and the writings of Thoreau. Civil disobedience, I argued, was essential to democracy when the ordinary channels of representative government were inadequate in the face of a terrible injustice.

To be a public intellectual is the most satisfying of endeavors. It is a proper role for someone who loves ideas and the transmission of ideas, but who does not want to be isolated in the library or the classroom while the cities burn and people go homeless and the violence of war ravages whole continents.

Suggested Reading

Lynd R S (1939) *Knowledge for What?* Princeton: Princeton University Press.
Wright Mills C (1959) *The Sociological Imagination.* Oxford: Oxford University Press.
Chomsky N (1969) *American Power and the New Mandarins.* London: Chatto and Windus.
Zinn H (1994) *You Can't Be Neutral on a Moving Train.* Boston: Beacon.

Chapter 20
When Theory Meets Politics

Doreen Massey

"¿Viste?... el cuarto motor... ¿viste?"
[Did you see?... the fourth motor... did you see?]
The guy in the back of the car is gesticulating and laughing, but it is too late. I haven't seen it. But I want to. So we cut off the main road to circle back, to try to pass it again; we get lost in a maze of small streets, one-ways going the wrong way, and culs-de-sac. Finally we make it back on to the main road and drive by again, slowly this time, so that I, giving full rein to self-indulgence, can take photographs.

We are in Caracas, Venezuela. It is September 2007 and political contest is everywhere. What we had passed was a huge, red hoarding, one of many draping the city, arguing the case for the Bolivarian revolution and for the next steps to be taken to push it forward. On my way into the city, through the mountains from the narrow strip of coastal plain to which the airport clings, I'd already seen, slung across a whole block of flats, "Rumbo al Socialismo Bolivariano", and everywhere were invocations of "Todo el poder al pueblo". But there was also a more detailed, almost pedagogical, series of hoardings, spelling out "the five motors of the revolution". Some listed all five; others proclaimed just one. And what we had just passed was a huge announcement for the fourth: "La Nueva Geometría del Poder". The new power geometry. This is a concept I've been arguing for, and trying to work with for some years, and now here it is, in huge letters, and at the heart of one of the most radical of attempts to shift the balance of power, to re-imagine society, in a Latin America that is, once again, trying to re-invent itself and to refuse its supposed destiny of subordination to the imperium in the North. Clearly, this engagement as a "public intellectual" is going to be different from anything I've tried before.[1]

There are many different ways of being a "public scholar". I have been drawn into just a few, but each has demanded to be thought through in its own specific terms. Venturing beyond the confines of academe involves linking up with another assemblage of concerns, interests and aims, in which your position has to be negotiated. What will be your role? What will be your voice? And what will be the degree and nature of the responsibility to which you commit yourself? These questions are in part pragmatic and practical; but they are also a matter, in themselves, of politics and political responsibility. They also complicate, and often challenge, the official discourses of "dissemination", "application", "relevance", and "impact".

Perhaps one of the simplest ways of putting a toe out beyond the door of the academy is addressing wider audiences. For me, this has included writing for, or working on the editorial boards of, a range of political magazines (*Marxism Today, Capital and Class, New Left Review* among others), doing talks or lectures or discussions in non-academic settings, and contributing to radio and television. It can include proseletysing for "geography" (the importance of the spatial, for instance), or contributing to political debates; even teaching sometimes, because I work at the Open University—a university dedicated to popular education, for which there are no entry qualifications—can have this flavour too. That ideas are not just "academic", where academic becomes synonymous with irrelevant ("oh that's just academic") but part of the medium in which we live, that they should be shared and more widely shared. Popular education as a component of democracy.

At one level, this kind of engagement can be seen simply as "getting our message across" and in the UK, in the guise of "dissemination", it has been incorporated into the standard practices of evaluation of academic work. In forms to apply for, or report on, research you will be enjoined to say, in a little box, how your work is "relevant", and to which constituencies. It is part of a wider effort to make universities "useful" and has its own double-edgedness. Originally, "they" had in mind, as the recipients of our relevance, the makers of public policy and the entrepreneurs of the business world. Later (I write of the UK) they learned from the grumblings and recalcitrances of (I suspect mainly) social scientists, and this "audience" was broadened (voluntary agencies, trades unions). It is interesting to see how far this can be pushed—to cite, for instance, some group in the World Social Forum as the primary beneficiary of one's "relevance".

The implicit geography behind much of this form of public engagement is that the communication is one way. The term "dissemination" makes that clear; it mirrors those projects for "the public understanding of science". The assumed positioning is evident, there is no need for negotiation: we tell them. And yet it can be (should be?) almost always also more than that. The question from an unexpected angle, that long discussion you had afterwards. The thoughts you carried home. This is perhaps especially true because for me being a "public intellectual" has often meant specifically political engagement. (I don't think it *has* to, but it is so for me.) Moreover political commitment raises other questions of self-positioning and responsibility, and yet more awkward intersections with the language of academic governance.

As well as "disseminating", UK academics are also required to demonstrate how our work can be "applied" and what "impact" it has had.[2] Again the implication is of a simple, unproblematic, and one-way, relation.

One means of having influence in the political field is through direct policy engagement. I have tried this in various ways, with different degrees of satisfaction and success. I was, just to give one example, for much of the 1970s an "expert" on a Labour Party policy committee. There were two crucial things to be negotiated here. First, politically speaking, I came from a different planet, and thus much thought and care had to go into developing a voice that might at least have some traction in the discussion. However, apart from the problem of political position, there was also a "culture" to negotiate. This group was by no means the worst I've come across, but what it seemed to want most from its participants was gravitas, not to say portentousness. Apart from my gut resistance to this in any case, it is difficult to exude gravitas when you're 5 ft 1 and the committee room table comes up to your chin, when you're blond, and a GIRL, who is not even wearing a suit. Throughout my intermittent attempts to engage with "the establishment" of this country I have been left in no doubt that your ideas are evaluated through a filter, unacknowledged and often unintended, of expectation of a particular kind of embodiment. You can play the required female game and smile a lot, or you can adopt a deportment that says you take yourself very, very seriously. There is a self-importance that brings out in me an overwhelming desire to prick it. It is itself a form of class and gender war.

But the issue of politics is paramount. How could any of us from even the broadest of broad lefts expect to have any policy "impact" on the rampaging Thatcher government? The very *possibility* of "impact" is two way. And although there is sometimes an implicit supposition that our advice will be "technical" (ie politically neutral), it is of course rarely so, nor expected—actually—to be so. Even in the era when New Labour was rabbitting on about evidence-led policy, they frequently rejected evidence that went against their already-held positions. Or they framed questions you couldn't possibly answer because you didn't see the world that way in the first place.

But there are other ways, more and less direct, of engaging with policy and politics. The more direct way is to engage in the policy-making process itself, when a political situation arises where this is possible: when you get the chance to engage with a "government" that is actually working for the kind of world you might want to live in. In the 1980s I was a member of the Board of the Greater London Enterprise Board, the economic policy arm of the left-wing Greater London Council (GLC). It is salutary, and politically important I think, not always to be in a position of critic (I think of all the easy, anti-State stuff, and sniping from "the margins"—which academics rarely inhabit—that litters much theoretical and "critical" writing); to be forced to be constructive and to take a different kind of responsibility (including responsibility for compromises). This kind of engagement, in the immediacy and implacable reality of a decision-making process, proved to me beyond doubt that the notion of "applied work" is in these situations utterly inadequate. The notion of "application" presumes a classic linear model: first you do the theory, have the ideas, then you go out and inflict them upon the world. No way. Some of the moments most disruptive to my existing way of thinking have been in precisely such engagements; and that provocation to reconceptualise has continued through the subsequent decades of my involvement with London politics (Massey 2007).

The "less direct" way of engaging politically as an academic has been through active participation in struggles and campaigns and through contributing to wider debate in civil society. In 1995, Michael Rustin, Stuart Hall and I founded a magazine: *Soundings: A Journal of Politics and Culture*.[3] It sprang from our frustration at the vacuity of political debate. This was the fag-end of the Thatcher/Major era; it was plain that the Conservatives were going to lose office; it was also plain that there needed to be debate about what would succeed them. *Soundings* is not "academic" (at one point we thought of jokily subtitling it "a non-refereed journal"), but it is somehow no accident that the three founders work in universities and that a high proportion of its contributors do so too. As well as the journal, the project involves seminars, networks, conferences. Communication is certainly not one way.

Moreover in these meetings—I'm thinking, for instance, of a heated discussion one Saturday afternoon about whether Brown would be any better than Blair, and how, if at all, one should engage—I'm not there as a "public scholar" but as a politically engaged person who happens to (have the luck to) work in a university. For me, in the UK in a context where the change you want to work towards is so much more radical than currently hegemonic agendas, it has been this longer haul, of trying to shift debate, to change its terms, rather than some immediate effect on policy, that has been the most honest and sympathetic.

Being involved in ongoing political struggles means, each time, re-negotiating the nature of one's involvement and responsibility. This I have found to be particularly acute in engagements outside my own country. Two brief examples.

After the release of Mandela, in the early years of ANC government, I was invited to participate in debates about what should be the regional organisation of South Africa. This opportunity meant linking in to a history in which I had not been part, into a geography of struggles in which I was clearly not "expert", into debates where particular words could let loose bounding chains of connotations that I could not know about, and a situation where I was white and from "the West". What role can you play? Many have written about this (Spivak is one obvious contributor) and there is no space here for a serious discussion. (In a comradely and welcoming group in the new South Africa I worked out something around being able to use my own experience to ask questions, even awkward ones, within an assumption of political solidarity.) The only point I want to make here is that this thinking about, and negotiation of, one's positioning is the toughest part of the whole thing.

And so again in Caracas the same questions arise as to how to respond to the invitation: questions of voice and stance and role. I am to do lectures, television stuff, public political meetings . . . (And in a Spanish learned for 1980s Nicaragua, with the Sandinistas in government and Reagan's Contra waging war; while back home Thatcher was preparing to abolish the GLC. How things come round.) But here in Venezuela there are more complexities. This concept (of "mine") has travelled, been adopted by Chávez. It's being used in a particular way. What responsibilities does one have in a situation like this? Whose concept is it now? The best, minimalist, way may be not to insist on anything, but to aim to enrich discussion through elaboration ("what I was trying to get at when I came up with this idea . . ."; "the way I've tried to use it . . ."; "the kind of thing it can be used for in the UK . . ."). Yet inexorably one becomes part of the politics of this place ("well I think it needs to be used in the economic as well as the political sphere . . ."; "you have to look here at the balance between centralisation and popular power . . ."). One of the many impressive aspects of the Bolivarian revolution is its active and explicit use of "ideas". Chávez on television and in meetings reads passages from "academic" tomes, and then meditates on them, live, trying to draw out thoughts that might be relevant to building "a socialism for the 21st century". The works of Hardt and Negri, and of Laclau, amongst many others, are drawn on extensively. The concept of multitude resonates strongly in a country long ruled by an oligarchy separated by a chasm of wealth, power, and the self-enclosures of mutual ignorance, from the mass of the impoverished. The concept of hegemony and a reformulation in that light of the notion of populism helps think through a conjuncture in which the legitimacy of the formal state apparatus has pretty much collapsed. It is utterly invigorating to be in a situation where ideas really matter. But also one where they are not simply taken as "truth". Concepts are drawn on and reworked in the complexity of the actual situation. This is part of that long Latin American endeavour of developing a voice of its own. The different theories/concepts anyway interrupt each other. (I am engaged in a demanding debate about how to (indeed can you?) work with Negri and Laclau together.) I am totally at one with this; it is after all an argument about geographical specificity. It means you "let go" of "your" concept (power geometry, say) at the same time as trying to insert into the debate the aspects that, you think, for now, provisionally, might be essential. (I have to stop myself falling again into anger at the CV-enhancing stuff that sometimes passes for theoretical engagement back home, so often written of as "risky" even "dangerous", before the authors return to their oh-so-conventional lives.) Sometimes you're running after the concept, trying to keep up, and learning. I am told that on the streets in some parts of Caracas there is talk of "la geometría del poder *popular*". There are other ways too, but for me this, along with the hard and lengthy reflection and rumination that come afterwards, is how "theory" develops; and this is how it can matter.

Endnotes

[1] The motors concern (i) enabling legislation, (ii) constitutional reform, (iii) education, (iv) a new power geometry (political territorialisation), (v) development of popular power.

[2] "Applied" work is imagined as distinct from theoretical and has, in this age in which we are enjoined to be useful, become more fashionable at least in the formal criteria for evaluation—closetly, in the private imaginations of many, it still carries less esteem. "Impact" may be within or beyond the academy.

[3] http://www.lwbooks.co.uk/journals/soundings

Reference

Massey D (2007) *World City*. Cambridge: Polity.

Index